THE
RETURN OF
THE PRODIGAL SON

OTHER BOOKS BY HENRI J. M. NOUWEN

THE
RETURN
OF THE
PRODIGAL
SON

.

A Story of
Homecoming

Henri J. M. Nouwen

IMAGE BOOKS
Doubleday
NEW YORK   LONDON   TORONTO   SYDNEY   AUCKLAND

To my father
Laurent Jean Marie Nouwen
for his ninetieth birthday

AN IMAGE BOOK
PUBLISHED BY DOUBLEDAY
a division of Bantam Doubleday Dell Publishing Group, Inc.
1540 Broadway, New York, New York 10036

IMAGE, DOUBLEDAY, and the portrayal of a deer drinking
from a stream are trademarks of Doubleday,
a division of Bantam Doubleday Dell Publishing Group, Inc.

First Image Books edition published April 1994
by special arrangement with Doubleday.

Library of Congress Cataloging-in-Publication Data
Nouwen, Henri J. M.
  The return of the prodigal son: a story of home-
coming / Henri J. M. Nouwen.
      p. cm.
  Originally published: New York: Doubleday, 1992.
  Includes bibliographical references.
  1. Spiritual life—Catholic church.   2. Rembrandt
Harmenszoon van Rijn, 1606-1669. Return of the
prodigal son.   3. Nouwen, Henri J. M.   I. Title.
[BX2350.2.N667 1993]   93-33836
248.4'82—dc20   CIP

ISBN 0-385-47307-9

26 28 30 29 27

CONTENTS

■

The Story of Two Sons and Their Father

·

There was a man who had two sons. The younger one said to his father, "Father, let me have the share of the estate that will come to me." So the father divided the property between them. A few days later, the younger son got together everything he had and left for a distant country where he squandered his money on a life of debauchery.

When he had spent it all, that country experienced a severe famine, and now he began to feel the pinch so he hired himself out to one of the local inhabitants who put him on his farm to feed the pigs. And he would willingly have filled himself with the husks the pigs were eating but no one would let him have them. Then he came to his senses and said, "How many of my father's hired men have all the food they want and more, and here am I dying of hunger! I will leave this place and go to my father and say: Father, I have sinned against heaven and against you; I no longer deserve to be called your son; treat me as one of your hired men. . . ." So he left the place and went back to his father.

While he was still a long way off, his father saw him and was moved with pity. He ran to the boy, clasped him in his arms and kissed him. Then his son said, "Father, I have sinned against heaven and against you. I no longer deserve to be called your son." But the father said to his servants, "Quick! Bring out the best robe and put it on him; put a ring on his finger and sandals on his feet. Bring the calf we have been fattening, and kill it; we will celebrate by having a feast, because this son of mine was dead and has come back to life; he was lost and is found." And they began to celebrate.

Now the elder son was out in the fields, and on his way back, as he drew near the house, he could hear music and dancing. Calling one of the servants he asked what it was all about. The servant told him, "Your brother has come, and your father has killed the calf we had been fattening because he has got him back safe and sound." He was angry then and refused to go in, and his father came out and began to urge him to come in; but he retorted to his father, "All these years I have slaved for you and never once disobeyed any orders of yours, yet you never offered me so much as a kid for me to celebrate with my friends. But, for this son of yours, when he comes back after swallowing up your property—he and his loose women— you kill the calf we had been fattening."

The father said, "My son, you are with me always, and all I have is yours. But it was only right we should celebrate and rejoice, be- cause your brother here was dead and has come to life; he was lost and is found."

PROLOGUE:
ENCOUNTER WITH A
PAINTING

.

The Poster

A seemingly insignificant encounter with a poster presenting a detail of Rembrandt's *The Return of the Prodigal Son* set in motion a long spiritual adventure that brought me to a new understanding of my vocation and offered me new strength to live it. At the heart of this adventure is a seventeenth-century painting and its artist, a first-century parable and its author, and a twentieth-century person in search of life's meaning.

The story begins in the fall of 1983 in the village of Trosly, France, where I was spending a few months at L'Arche, a community that offers a home to people with mental handicaps. Founded in

1964 by a Canadian, Jean Vanier, the Trosly community is the first of more than ninety L'Arche communities spread throughout the world.

One day I went to visit my friend Simone Landrien in the community's small documentation center. As we spoke, my eyes fell on a large poster pinned on her door. I saw a man in a great red cloak tenderly touching the shoulders of a disheveled boy kneeling before him. I could not take my eyes away. I felt drawn by the intimacy between the two figures, the warm red of the man's cloak, the golden yellow of the boy's tunic, and the mysterious light engulfing them both. But, most of all, it was the hands—the old man's hands—as they touched the boy's shoulders that reached me in a place where I had never been reached before.

Realizing that I was no longer paying much attention to the conversation, I said to Simone, "Tell me about that poster." She said, "Oh, that's a reproduction of Rembrandt's *Prodigal Son*. Do you like it?" I kept staring at the poster and finally stuttered, "It's beautiful, more than beautiful . . . it makes me want to cry and laugh at the same time . . . I can't tell you what I feel as I look at it, but it touches me deeply." Simone said, "Maybe you should have your own copy. You can buy it in Paris." "Yes," I said, "I must have a copy."

When I first saw the *Prodigal Son,* I had just finished an exhausting six-week lecturing trip through the United States, calling Christian communities to do anything they possibly could to prevent violence and war in Central America. I was dead tired, so much so that I could barely walk. I was anxious, lonely, restless, and very needy. During the trip I had felt like a strong fighter for justice and peace, able to face the dark world without fear. But after it was all over I felt like a vulnerable little child who wanted to crawl onto its mother's lap and cry. As soon as the cheering or cursing crowds were gone, I experienced a devastating loneliness and could easily have surrendered myself to the seductive voices that promised emotional and physical rest.

It was in this condition that I first encountered Rembrandt's

Prodigal Son on the door of Simone's office. My heart leapt when I saw it. After my long self-exposing journey, the tender embrace of father and son expressed everything I desired at that moment. I was, indeed, the son exhausted from long travels; I wanted to be embraced; I was looking for a home where I could feel safe. The son-come-home was all I was and all that I wanted to be. For so long I had been going from place to place: confronting, beseeching, admonishing, and consoling. Now I desired only to rest safely in a place where I could feel a sense of belonging, a place where I could feel at home.

Much happened in the months and years that followed. Even though the extreme fatigue left me and I returned to a life of teaching and traveling, Rembrandt's embrace remained imprinted on my soul far more profoundly than any temporary expression of emotional support. It had brought me into touch with something within me that lies far beyond the ups and downs of a busy life, something that represents the ongoing yearning of the human spirit, the yearning for a final return, an unambiguous sense of safety, a lasting home. While busy with many people, involved in many issues, and quite visible in many places, the homecoming of the prodigal son stayed with me and continued to take on even greater significance in my spiritual life. The yearning for a lasting home, brought to consciousness by Rembrandt's painting, grew deeper and stronger, somehow making the painter himself into a faithful companion and guide.

Two years after first seeing the Rembrandt poster, I resigned from my teaching position at Harvard University and returned to L'Arche in Trosly, there to spend a full year. The purpose of this move was to determine whether or not I was called to live a life with mentally handicapped people in one of the L'Arche communities. During that year of transition, I felt especially close to Rembrandt and his *Prodigal Son*. After all, I was looking for a new home. It seemed as though my fellow Dutchman had been given to me as a special companion. Before the year was over, I had made the decision to make L'Arche my new home and to join Daybreak, the L'Arche community in Toronto.

The Painting

Just before leaving Trosly, I was invited by my friends Bobby Massie and his wife, Dana Robert, to join them on a trip to the Soviet Union. My immediate reaction was: "Now I can see the real painting." Ever since becoming interested in this great work, I had known that the original had been acquired in 1766 by Catherine the Great for the Hermitage in Saint Petersburg (which after the revolution was given the name of Leningrad, and which has recently reclaimed its original name of Saint Petersburg) and was still there. I never dreamt that I would have a chance to see it so soon. Although I was very eager to get firsthand knowledge of a country that had so strongly influenced my thoughts, emotions, and feelings during most of my life, this became almost trivial when compared with the opportunity to sit before the painting that had revealed to me the deepest yearnings of my heart.

From the moment of my departure, I knew that my decision to join L'Arche on a permanent basis and my visit to the Soviet Union were closely linked. The link—I was sure—was Rembrandt's *Prodigal Son*. Somehow, I sensed that seeing this painting would allow me to enter into the mystery of homecoming in a way I never had before.

Returning from an exhausting lecture tour to a safe place had been a homecoming; leaving the world of teachers and students to live in a community for mentally handicapped men and women felt like returning home; meeting the people of a country which had separated itself from the rest of the world by walls and heavily guarded borders, that, too, was, in its own way, a manner of going home. But, beneath or beyond all that, "coming home" meant, for me, walking step by step toward the One who awaits me with open arms and wants to hold me in an eternal embrace. I knew that Rembrandt deeply understood this spiritual homecoming. I knew that, when Rembrandt painted his *Prodigal Son,* he had lived a life that had left him with no doubt about his true and final home. I felt that, if I could meet Rembrandt right where he had painted father and son, God and humanity, compassion and misery, in one circle of love, I would come to know as much as I ever would about death and life. I also sensed the hope that through Rembrandt's masterpiece I would one day be able to express what I most wanted to say about love.

Being in Saint Petersburg is one thing. Having the opportunity to quietly reflect upon the *Prodigal Son* in the Hermitage is quite something else. When I saw the mile-long line of people waiting to enter the museum, I wondered anxiously how and for how long I would be able to see what I most wanted to see.

My anxiety, however, was relieved. In Saint Petersburg our official tour ended, and most members of the group returned home. But Bobby's mother, Suzanne Massie, who was in the Soviet Union during our trip, invited us to stay a few days with her. Suzanne is an expert in Russian culture and art, and her book *The Land of the Firebird* had greatly helped me to get ready for our trip. I asked Suzanne, "How do I ever get close to the *Prodigal Son?*" She said, "Now, Henri, don't worry. I'll see to it that you have all the time you want and need with your favorite painting."

During our second day in Saint Petersburg, Suzanne gave me a telephone number and said, "This is the office number of Alexei Briantsev. He is a good friend of mine. Call him, and he will help you to get to your *Prodigal Son.*" I dialed the number immediately and was surprised to hear Alexei, in his gently accented English, promise to meet me at a side door, away from the tourist entrance.

On Saturday, July 26, 1986, at 2:30 P.M., I went to the Hermitage, walked along the Neva River past the main entrance, and found the door Alexei had directed me to. I entered, and someone behind a large desk let me use the house phone to call Alexei. After a few minutes, he appeared and welcomed me with great kindness. He led me along splendid corridors and elegant staircases to an out-of-the-way place not on the tourists' itinerary. It was a long room with high ceilings and looked like an old artist's studio. Paintings were stacked everywhere. In the middle there were large tables and chairs covered with papers and objects of all sorts. As we sat down for a moment, it soon became clear to me that Alexei was the head of the Hermitage's restoration department. With great gentleness and obvious interest in my desire to spend time with Rembrandt's painting, he offered me all the help I wanted. Then he took me straight to the *Prodigal Son,* told the guard not to bother me, and left me there.

And so there I was; facing the painting that had been on my mind and in my heart for nearly three years. I was stunned by its majestic beauty. Its size, larger than life; its abundant reds, browns, and yellows; its shadowy recesses and bright foreground, but most of all the light-enveloped embrace of father and son surrounded by four mysterious bystanders, all of this gripped me with an intensity far beyond my anticipation. There had been moments in which I had wondered whether the real painting might disappoint me. The opposite was true. Its grandeur and splendor made everything recede into the background and held me completely captivated. Coming here was indeed a homecoming.

While many tourist groups with their guides came and left in rapid succession, I sat on one of the red velvet chairs in front of the painting and just looked. Now I was seeing the real thing! Not only the father embracing his child-come-home, but also the elder son and the three other figures. It is a huge work in oil on canvas, eight feet high by six feet wide. It took me a while to simply *be* there, simply absorbing that I was truly in the presence of what I had so long hoped to see, simply enjoying the fact that I was all by myself sitting in the Hermitage in Saint Petersburg looking at the *Prodigal Son* for as long as I wanted.

The painting was exposed in the most favorable way, on a wall that received plenty of natural light through a large nearby window at an eighty-degree angle. Sitting there, I realized that the light became fuller and more intense as the afternoon progressed. At four o'clock the sun covered the painting with a new brightness, and the background figures—which had remained quite vague in the early hours —seemed to step out of their dark corners. As the evening drew near, the sunlight grew more crisp and tingling. The embrace of the father and son became stronger and deeper, and the bystanders participated more directly in this mysterious event of reconciliation, forgiveness, and inner healing. Gradually I realized that there were as many paintings of the *Prodigal Son* as there were changes in the light, and, for a long time, I was held spellbound by this gracious dance of nature and art.

Without my realizing it, more than two hours had gone by when Alexei reappeared. With a compassionate smile and a supportive gesture, he suggested that I needed a break and invited me for coffee. He led me through the majestic halls of the museum—the larger part of which was the old winter palace of the tsars—back to the work space where we had been before. Alexei and his colleague had set out a large spread of breads, cheeses, and sweets, and encouraged me to enjoy it all. Having afternoon coffee with the art restorers of the Hermitage was certainly not what I had dreamt about when I was hoping to spend some quiet time with the *Prodigal Son*. Both Alexei and his colleague shared with me all they knew about Rembrandt's painting and were very eager to know why I was so taken by it. They seemed surprised and even a bit perplexed by my spiritual observations and reflections. They listened attentively and urged me to tell more.

After coffee, I returned to the painting for another hour until the guard and the cleaning lady let me know, in no uncertain terms, that the museum was closing and that I had been there long enough.

Four days later, I returned for another visit to the painting. During that session, something amusing happened, something that I should not leave untold. Because of the angle from which the morning sun hit the painting, the varnish gave off a distracting glare. So I took one of the red velvet chairs and moved it to a place from which the glare was cut and I could once again see clearly the figures in the painting. As soon as the guard—a serious young man with cap and military-type uniform—saw what I was doing, he became very upset at my audacity in picking up my chair and putting it somewhere else. Walking up to me, he ordered me, with an outpouring of Russian words and universal gestures, to put the chair back in its place. In response, I pointed to the sun and the canvas, trying to explain to him why I had moved the chair. My efforts had absolutely no success. So I returned the chair to its place and sat on the floor instead. But that only disturbed the guard even more. After some further animated attempts to win the sympathy of the guard for my problem, he told me to sit on the radiator below the window, from where I could have a good view. However, the first Intourist guide passing by with a large group marched up to me and told me sternly to get off the radiator and sit on one of the velvet chairs. At that, the guard became very angry at the guide and told her with a profusion of words and gestures that it was he who had let me sit on the radiator. The guide did not seem satisfied but decided to return her attention to the tourists, who were looking at the Rembrandt and wondering about the size of the figures. A few minutes later, Alexei came to see how I was doing. Immediately, the guard walked up to him and both of them entered into a long conversation. The guard was obviously trying to explain what had happened, but the discussion lasted so long that I wondered somewhat anxiously where it all would lead. Then, quite suddenly, Alexei left. For a moment, I felt quite guilty at having caused such a stir and thought that I had made Alexei angry with me. Ten minutes later, however, Alexei returned carrying a large comfortable armchair with red velvet upholstery and gold-painted legs. All for me! With a big grin, he put the chair in front of the painting and bade me sit in it. Alexei, the guard, and I all smiled. I had my own chair, and nobody objected any longer. Suddenly it all seemed very comical. Three empty chairs that could not be touched and a luxurious armchair brought in from some other room in the winter palace, offered to me to be freely moved around. Elegant bureaucracy! I wondered if any of the figures in the painting, who had been witnesses to the whole scene, were smiling along with us. I will never know.

Altogether, I spent more than four hours with the *Prodigal Son*, making notes about what I heard the guides and the tourists say, about what I saw as the sun grew stronger and faded away, and about what I experienced in my innermost being as I became more and more part of the story that Jesus once told and Rembrandt once painted. I wondered whether and how these precious hours in the Hermitage would ever bear fruit.

When I left the painting, I walked up to the young guard and tried to express my gratitude for his putting up with me for so long. As I looked into his eyes under the large Russian cap, I saw a man like myself: afraid, but with a great desire to be forgiven. From his beardless young face came a very gentle smile. I smiled too, and the two of us felt safe.

The Event

A few weeks after visiting the Hermitage in Saint Petersburg, I arrived at L'Arche Daybreak in Toronto to live and work as the pastor of the community. Although I had taken a full year to sort out my vocation and to discern whether God was calling me to a life with mentally handicapped people, I still felt very apprehensive and anxious about my ability to live it well. I had never before given much attention to people with a mental handicap. Much to the contrary, I had focused increasingly on university students and their problems. I learned how to give lectures and write books, how to explain things systematically, how to make titles and subtitles, how to argue and how to analyze. So I had little idea as to how to communicate with men and women who hardly speak and, if they do speak, are not interested in logical arguments or well-reasoned opinions. I knew even less about announcing the Gospel of Jesus to people who listened more with their hearts than with their minds and who were far more sensitive to what I lived than to what I said.

I came to Daybreak in August 1986, with the conviction that I had made the right choice, but with a heart still full of trepidation about what lay ahead of me. Despite this I was convinced that, after more than twenty years in the classroom, the time had come to trust that God loves the poor in spirit in a very special way and that—even though I may have had little to offer them—they had a lot to offer me.

One of the first things I did after my arrival was to look for a good place to hang my poster of the *Prodigal Son*. The work space that was given to me proved ideal. Whenever I sat down to read, write, or talk to someone, I could see that mysterious embrace of father and son that had become such an intimate part of my spiritual journey.

Since my visit to the Hermitage, I had become more aware of the four figures, two women and two men, who stood around the luminous space where the father welcomed his returning son. Their way of looking leaves you wondering how they think or feel about what they are watching. These bystanders, or observers, allow for all sorts of interpretations. As I reflect on my own journey, I become more and more aware of how long I have played the role of observer. For years I had instructed students on the different aspects of the spiritual life, trying to help them see the importance of living it. But had I, myself, really ever dared to step into the center, kneel down, and let myself be held by a forgiving God?

The simple fact of being able to express an opinion, to set up an argument, to defend a position, and to clarify a vision has given me, and gives me still, a sense of control. And, generally, I feel much safer in experiencing a sense of control over an undefinable situation than in taking the risk of letting that situation control me.

Certainly there were many hours of prayer, many days and months of retreat, and countless conversations with spiritual directors, but I had never fully given up the role of bystander. Even though there has been in me a lifelong desire to be an insider looking out, I nevertheless kept choosing over and over again the position of the outsider looking in. Sometimes this looking-in was a curious looking-in, sometimes a jealous looking-in, sometimes an anxious looking-in, and, once in a while, even a loving looking-in. But giving up the somewhat safe position of the critical observer seemed like a great leap into totally unknown territory. I so much wanted to keep some control over my spiritual journey, to remain able to predict at least a part of the outcome, that relinquishing the security of the observer for the vulnerability of the returning son seemed close to impossible. Teaching students, passing on the many explanations given over the centuries to the words and actions of Jesus, and showing them the many spiritual journeys that people have chosen in the past seemed very much like taking the position of one of the four figures surrounding the divine embrace. The two women standing behind the father at different distances, the seated man staring into space and looking at no one in particular, and the tall man standing erect and looking critically at the event on the platform in front of him—they all represent different ways of not getting involved. There is indifference, curiosity, daydreaming, and attentive observation; there is staring, gazing, watching, and looking; there is standing in the background, leaning against an arch, sitting with arms crossed, and standing with hands gripping each other. Every one of these inner and outer postures is all too familiar to me. Some are more comfortable than others, but all of them are ways of not getting directly involved.

Moving from teaching university students to living with mentally handicapped people was, for me at least, a step toward the platform where the father embraces his kneeling son. It is the place of light, the place of truth, the place of love. It is the place where I so much want to be, but am so fearful of being. It is the place where I will receive all I desire, all I ever hoped for, all that I will ever need, but it is also the place where I have to let go of all I most want to hold on to. It is the place that confronts me with the fact that truly accepting love, forgiveness, and healing is often much harder than giving it. It is the place beyond earning, deserving, and rewarding. It is the place of surrender and complete trust.

Soon after I came to Daybreak, Linda, a beautiful young woman with Down's syndrome, put her arms around me and said: "Welcome." She does that to every newcomer, and every time she does it, she does it with unreserved conviction and love. But how to receive such an embrace? Linda had never met me. She had no understanding at all of what I had lived before coming to Daybreak. She had never had the chance to encounter my dark side, nor to discover my corners of light. She had never read any of my books, heard me speak, or even had a decent conversation with me.

So, should I just smile, call her cute, and walk on as if nothing had happened? Or was Linda standing somewhere on the platform and saying with her gesture, "Come on up, don't be so bashful, your Father wants to hold you too!" It seems that every time—be it Linda's welcome, Bill's handshake, Gregory's smile, Adam's silence, or Raymond's words—I have to make a choice between "explaining" these gestures or simply accepting them as invitations to come higher up and closer by.

These years at Daybreak have not been easy. There has been much inner struggle, and there has been mental, emotional, and spiritual pain. Nothing, absolutely nothing, had about it the quality of having arrived. However, the move from Harvard to L'Arche proved to be but one little step from bystander to participant, from judge to repentant sinner, from teacher about love to being loved as the beloved. I really did not have an inkling of how difficult the journey would be. I did not realize how deeply rooted my resistance was and how agonizing it would be to "come to my senses," fall on my knees, and let my tears flow freely. I did not realize how hard it would be to become truly part of the great event that Rembrandt's painting portrays.

Each little step toward the center seemed like an impossible demand, a demand requiring me to let go one more time from wanting to be in control, to give up one more time the desire to predict life, to die one more time to the fear of not knowing where it all will lead, and to surrender one more time to a love that knows no limits. And still, I knew that I would never be able to live the great commandment to love without allowing myself to be loved without conditions or prerequisites. The journey from teaching about love to allowing myself to be loved proved much longer than I realized.

The Vision

Much of what has happened since my arrival at Daybreak is written down in diaries and notebooks, but, as it stands, little of it is fit to share with others. The words are too raw, too noisy, too "bloody," and too naked. But now a time has come when it is possible to look back on those years of turmoil and to describe, with more objectivity than was possible before, the place to which all of that struggle has brought me. I am still not free enough to let myself be held completely in the safe embrace of the Father. In many ways I am still moving toward the center. I am still like the prodigal: traveling, preparing speeches, anticipating how it will be when I finally reach my Father's house. But I am, indeed, on my way home. I have left the distant country and come to feel the nearness of love. And so, I am ready now to share my story. There is some hope, some light, some consolation to be found in it. Much of what I have lived in the past few years will be part of this story, not as an expression of confusion or despair, but as moments in my journey toward the light.

Rembrandt's painting has remained very close to me throughout this time. I have moved it around many times: from my office to the chapel, from the chapel to the living room of the Dayspring (the house of prayer at Daybreak), and from the living room of the Dayspring back to the chapel. I have spoken about it many times inside and outside of the Daybreak community: to handicapped people and their assistants, to ministers and priests, and to men and women from diverse walks of life. The more I spoke of the *Prodigal Son,* the more I came to see it as, somehow, my personal painting, the painting that contained not only the heart of the story that God wants to tell me, but also the heart of the story that I want to tell to God and God's people. All of the Gospel is there. All of my life is there. All of the lives of my friends is there. The painting has become a mysterious window through which I can step into the Kingdom of God. It is like a huge gate that allows me to move to the other side of existence and look from there back into the odd assortment of people and events that make up my daily life.

For many years I tried to get a glimpse of God by looking carefully at the varieties of human experience: loneliness and love, sorrow and joy, resentment and gratitude, war and peace. I sought to understand the ups and downs of the human soul, to discern there a hunger and thirst that only a God whose name is Love could satisfy. I tried to discover the lasting beyond the passing, the eternal beyond the temporal, the perfect love beyond all paralyzing fears, and the divine consolation beyond the desolation of human anguish and agony. I tried constantly to point beyond the mortal quality of our existence to a presence larger, deeper, wider, and more beautiful than we can imagine, and to speak about that presence as a presence that can already now be seen, heard, and touched by those who are willing to believe.

However, during my time here at Daybreak, I have been led to an inner place where I had not been before. It is the place within me where God has chosen to dwell. It is the place where I am held safe in the embrace of an all-loving Father who calls me by name and says, "You are my beloved son, on you my favor rests." It is the place where I can taste the joy and the peace that are not of this world.

This place had always been there. I had always been aware of it as the source of grace. But I had not been able to enter it and truly live there. Jesus says, "Anyone who loves me will keep my word and my Father will love him, and we shall come to him and make our home in him." These words have always impressed me deeply. I am God's home!

But it had always been very hard to experience the truth of these words. Yes, God dwells in my innermost being, but how could I accept Jesus' call: "Make your home in me as I make mine in you"? The invitation is clear and unambiguous. To make my home where God had made his, this is the great spiritual challenge. It seemed an impossible task.

With my thoughts, feelings, emotions, and passions, I was constantly away from the place where God had chosen to make home.

Coming home and staying there where God dwells, listening to the voice of truth and love, that was, indeed, the journey I most feared because I knew that God was a jealous lover who wanted every part of me all the time. When would I be ready to accept that kind of love?

God himself showed me the way. The emotional and physical crises that interrupted my busy life at Daybreak compelled me—with violent force—to return home and to look for God where God can be found—in my own inner sanctuary. I am unable to say that I have arrived; I never will in this life, because the way to God reaches far beyond the boundary of death. While it is a long and very demanding journey, it is also one full of wonderful surprises, often offering us a taste of the ultimate goal.

When I first saw Rembrandt's painting, I was not as familiar with the home of God within me as I am now. Nevertheless, my intense response to the father's embrace of his son told me that I was desperately searching for that inner place where I too could be held as safely as the young man in the painting. At the time, I did not foresee what it would take to come a few steps closer to that place. I am grateful for not having known in advance what God was planning for me. But I am grateful as well for the new place that has been opened in me through all the inner pain. I have a new vocation now. It is the vocation to speak and write from that place back into the many places of my own and other people's restless lives. I have to kneel before the Father, put my ear against his chest and listen, without interruption, to the heartbeat of God. Then, and only then, can I say carefully and very gently what I hear. I know now that I have to speak from eternity into time, from the lasting joy into the passing realities of our short existence in this world, from the house of love into the houses of fear, from God's abode into the dwellings of human beings. I am well aware of the enormity of this vocation. Still, I am confident that it is the only way for me. One could call it the "prophetic" vision: looking at people and this world through the eyes of God.

Is this a realistic possibility for a human being? More important:

Is it a true option for me? This is not an intellectual question. It is a question of vocation. I am called to enter into the inner sanctuary of my own being where God has chosen to dwell. The only way to that place is prayer, unceasing prayer. Many struggles and much pain can clear the way, but I am certain that only unceasing prayer can let me enter it.

INTRODUCTION:
THE YOUNGER SON,
THE ELDER SON, AND
THE FATHER

．

During the year after I first saw the *Prodigal Son,* my spiritual journey was marked by three phases which helped me to find the structure of my story.

The first phase was my experience of being the younger son. The long years of university teaching and the intense involvement in South and Central American affairs had left me feeling quite lost. I had wandered far and wide, met people with all sorts of life-styles and convictions, and become part of many movements. But at the end of it all, I felt homeless and very tired. When I saw the tender way in which the father touched the shoulders of his young son and held him close to his heart, I felt very deeply that I was that lost son and wanted to return, as he did, to be embraced as he was. For a long time I thought of myself as the prodigal son on his way home, anticipating the moment of being welcomed by my Father.

Then, quite unexpectedly, something in my perspective shifted. After my year in France and my visit to the Hermitage in Saint Petersburg, the feelings of desperation that had made me identify so strongly with the younger son moved to the background of my consciousness. I had made up my mind to go to Daybreak in Toronto and, as a result, felt more self-confident than before.

The second phase in my spiritual journey was initiated one evening while talking about Rembrandt's painting to Bart Gavigan, a friend from England who had come to know me quite intimately during the past year. While I explained to Bart how strongly I had been able to identify with the younger son, he looked at me quite intently and said, "I wonder if you are not more like the elder son." With these words he opened a new space within me.

Frankly, I had never thought of myself as the elder son, but once Bart confronted me with that possibility, countless ideas started running through my head. Beginning with the simple fact that I am, indeed, the eldest child in my own family, I came to see how I had lived a quite dutiful life. When I was six years old, I already wanted to become a priest and never changed my mind. I was born, baptized, confirmed, and ordained in the same church and had always been obedient to my parents, my teachers, my bishops, and my God. I had never run away from home, never wasted my time and money on sensual pursuits, and had never gotten lost in "debauchery and drunkenness." For my entire life I had been quite responsible, traditional, and homebound. But, with all of that, I may, in fact, have been just as lost as the younger son. I suddenly saw myself in a completely new way. I saw my jealousy, my anger, my touchiness, doggedness and sullenness, and, most of all, my subtle self-righteousness. I saw how much of a complainer I was and how much of my thinking and feeling was ridden with resentment. For a time it became impossible to see how I could ever have thought of myself as the younger son. I was the elder son for sure, but just as lost as his younger brother, even though I had stayed "home" all my life.

I had been working very hard on my father's farm, but had never fully tasted the joy of being at home. Instead of being grateful for all the privileges I had received, I had become a very resentful person: jealous of my younger brothers and sisters who had taken so many risks and were so warmly welcomed back. During my first year and a half at Daybreak, Bart's insightful remark continued to guide my inner life.

There was more to come. In the months following the celebration of the thirtieth anniversary of my ordination to the priesthood, I gradually entered into very dark interior places and began to experience immense inner anguish. I came to a point where I could no longer feel safe in my own community and had to leave to seek help in my struggle and to work directly on my inner healing. The few books I could take with me were all about Rembrandt and the parable of the prodigal son. While living in a rather isolated place, far away from my friends and community, I found great consolation in reading the tormented life of the great Dutch painter and learning more about the agonizing journey that ultimately had enabled him to paint this magnificent work.

For hours I looked at the splendid drawings and paintings he created in the midst of all his setbacks, disillusionment, and grief, and I came to understand how from his brush there emerged the figure of a nearly blind old man holding his son in a gesture of all-forgiving compassion. One must have died many deaths and cried many tears to have painted a portrait of God in such humility.

It was during this period of immense inner pain that another friend spoke the word that I most needed to hear and opened up the third phase of my spiritual journey. Sue Mosteller, who had been with the Daybreak community from the early seventies and had played an important role in bringing me there, had given me indispensable support when things had become difficult, and had encouraged me to struggle through whatever needed to be suffered to reach true inner freedom. When she visited me in my "hermitage" and spoke with me about the *Prodigal Son,* she said, "Whether you are the younger son or the elder son, you have to realize that you are called to become the father."

Her words struck me like a thunderbolt because, after all my years of living with the painting and looking at the old man holding his son, it had never occurred to me that the father was the one who expressed most fully my vocation in life.

Sue did not give me much chance to protest: "You have been looking for friends all your life; you have been craving for affection as long as I've known you; you have been interested in thousands of things; you have been begging for attention, appreciation, and affirmation left and right. The time has come to claim your true vocation —to be a father who can welcome his children home without asking them any questions and without wanting anything from them in return. Look at the father in your painting and you will know who you are called to be. We, at Daybreak, and most people around you don't need you to be a good friend or even a kind brother. We need you to be a father who can claim for himself the authority of true compassion."

Looking at the bearded old man with his full red cloak, I felt deep resistance to thinking about myself in that way. I felt quite ready to identify myself with the spendthrift younger son or the resentful elder son, but the idea of being like the old man who had nothing to lose because he had lost all, and only to give, overwhelmed me with fear. Nevertheless, Rembrandt died when he was sixty-three years old and I am a lot closer to that age than to the age of either of the two sons. Rembrandt was willing to put himself in the father's place; why not I?

The year and a half since Sue Mosteller's challenge has been a time to begin claiming my spiritual fatherhood. It has been a slow and arduous struggle, and sometimes I still feel the desire to remain the son and never to grow old. But I also have tasted the immense joy of children coming home and of laying hands on them in a gesture of forgiveness and blessing. I have come to know in a small way what it means to be a father who asks no questions, wanting only to welcome his children home.

All that I have lived since my first encounter with the Rembrandt poster has not only given me the inspiration to write this book, but also suggested its structure. I will first reflect upon the younger son, then upon the elder son, and ultimately upon the father. For, indeed, I am the younger son; I am the elder son; and I am on my way to becoming the father. And for you who will make this spiritual journey with me, I hope and pray that you too will discover within yourselves not only the lost children of God, but also the compassionate mother and father that is God.

Part I

•

THE

YOUNGER
SON

The younger son said to his father, "Father, let me have the share of the estate that will come to me." So the father divided the property between them. A few days later, the younger son got together everything he had and left for a distant country where he squandered his money on a life of debauchery.

When he had spent it all, that country experienced a severe famine, and now he began to feel the pinch so he hired himself out to one of the local inhabitants who put him on his farm to feed the pigs. And he would willingly have filled himself with the husks the pigs were eating but no one would let him have them. Then he came to his senses and said, "How many of my father's hired men have all the food they want and more, and here am I dying of hunger! I will leave this place and go to my father and say: Father, I have sinned against heaven and against you; I no longer deserve to be called your son; treat me as one of your hired men." So he left the place and went back to his father.

I.

REMBRANDT
AND THE
YOUNGER SON

Rembrandt was close to his death when he painted his *Prodigal Son*. Most likely it was one of Rembrandt's last works. The more I read about it and look at it, the more I see it as a final statement of a tumultuous and tormented life. Together with his unfinished painting *Simeon and the Child Jesus*, the *Prodigal Son* shows the painter's perception of his aged self—a perception in which physical blindness and a deep inner seeing are intimately connected. The way in which the old Simeon holds the vulnerable child and the way in which the old father embraces his exhausted son reveal an inner vision that reminds one of Jesus' words to his disciples: "Blessed are the eyes that see what you see." Both Simeon and the father of the returning son carry *within* themselves that mysterious light by which they see. It is an inner light, deeply hidden, but radiating an all-pervasive tender beauty.

This inner light, however, had remained hidden for a long time. For many years it remained unreachable for Rembrandt. Only gradually and through much anguish did he come to know that light within himself and, through himself, in those he painted. Before being like the father, Rembrandt was for a long time like the proud young man who "got together everything he had and left for a distant country where he squandered his money."

When I look at the profoundly interiorized self-portraits which Rembrandt produced during his last years and which explain much of his ability to paint the luminous old father and the old Simeon, I must not forget that, as a young man, Rembrandt had all the characteristics of the prodigal son: brash, self-confident, spendthrift, sensual, and very arrogant. At the age of thirty, he painted himself with his wife, Saskia, as the lost son in a brothel. No interiority is visible there. Drunk, with his half-open mouth and sexually greedy eyes, he glares scornfully at those who look at his portrait as if to say: "Isn't this a lot of fun!" With his right hand he lifts up a half-empty glass, while with his left he touches the lower back of his girl whose eyes are no less lustful than his own. Rembrandt's long, curly hair, his velvet cap with the huge white feather, and the leather-sheathed sword with golden hilt touching the backs of the two merrymakers leave little doubt about their intentions. The drawn curtain in the upper right corner even makes one think of the brothels in Amsterdam's infamous red-light district. Gazing intently at this sensuous self-portrait of the young Rembrandt as the prodigal son, I can scarcely believe that this is the same man who, thirty years later, painted himself with eyes that penetrate so deeply into the hidden mysteries of life.

Still, all the Rembrandt biographers describe him as a proud young man, strongly convinced of his own genius and eager to explore everything the world has to offer; an extrovert who loves lux-

ury and is quite insensitive toward those about him. There is no doubt that one of Rembrandt's main concerns was money. He made a lot, he spent a lot, and he lost a lot. A large part of his energy was wasted in long, drawn-out court cases about financial settlements and bankruptcy proceedings. The self-portraits painted during his late twenties and early thirties reveal Rembrandt as a man hungry for fame and adulation, fond of extravagant costumes, preferring golden chains to the traditional starched white collars, and sporting outlandish hats, berets, helmets, and turbans. Although much of this elaborate dressing-up can be explained as a normal way to practice and show off painting techniques, it also demonstrates an arrogant character who wasn't simply out to please his sponsors.

However, this short period of success, popularity, and wealth is followed by much grief, misfortune, and disaster. Trying to summarize the many misfortunes of Rembrandt's life can be overwhelming. They are not unlike those of the prodigal son. After having lost his son Rumbartus in 1635, his first daughter Cornelia in 1638, and his second daughter Cornelia in 1640, Rembrandt's wife Saskia, whom he deeply loved and admired, dies in 1642. Rembrandt is left behind with his nine-month-old son, Titus. After Saskia's death, Rembrandt's life continues to be marked with countless pains and problems. A very unhappy relationship with Titus' nurse, Geertje Dircx, ending in lawsuits and the confinement of Geertje in an asylum, is followed by a more stable union with Hendrickje Stoffels. She bears him a son who dies in 1652 and a daughter, Cornelia, the only child who will survive him.

During these years, Rembrandt's popularity as a painter plummeted, even though some collectors and critics continued to recognize him as one of the greatest painters of the time. His financial problems became so severe that in 1656 Rembrandt is declared insolvent and asks for the right to sign over all his property and effects for the benefit of his creditors to avoid bankruptcy. All of Rembrandt's possessions, his own and other painters' works, his large collection of artifacts, his house in Amsterdam and his furniture, are sold in three auctions during 1657 and 1658.

Although Rembrandt would never become completely free of debt and debtors, in his early fifties he is able to find a modicum of peace. The increasing warmth and interiority of his paintings during this period show that the many disillusionments did not embitter him. On the contrary, they had a purifying effect on his way of seeing. Jakob Rosenberg writes: "He began to regard man and nature with an even more penetrating eye, no longer distracted by outward splendor or theatrical display." In 1663, Hendrickje dies, and five years later, Rembrandt witnesses not only the marriage but also the death of his beloved son, Titus. When Rembrandt himself dies in 1669, he has become a poor and lonely man. Only his daughter Cornelia, his daughter-in-law Magdalene van Loo, and his granddaughter Titia survived him.

As I look at the prodigal son kneeling before his father and pressing his face against his chest, I cannot but see there the once so self-confident and venerated artist who has come to the painful realization that all the glory he had gathered for himself proved to be vain glory. Instead of the rich garments with which the youthful Rembrandt painted himself in the brothel, he now wears only a torn undertunic covering his emaciated body, and the sandals, in which he had walked so far, have become worn out and useless.

Moving my eyes from the repentant son to the compassionate father, I see that the glittering light reflecting from golden chains, harnesses, helmets, candles, and hidden lamps has died out and been replaced by the inner light of old age. It is the movement from the glory that seduces one into an ever greater search for wealth and popularity to the glory that is hidden in the human soul and surpasses death.

2.

THE
YOUNGER SON
LEAVES

The younger one said to his father, "Father, let me have the share of the estate that will come to me." So the father divided the property between them. A few days later, the younger son got together everything he had and left for a distant country.

A Radical Rejection

The full title of Rembrandt's painting is, as has been said, *The Return of the Prodigal Son*. Implicit in the "return" is a leaving. Returning is a homecoming after a home-leaving, a coming back after having gone away. The father who welcomes his son home is so glad because this son "was dead and has come back to life; he was lost and is found." The immense joy in welcoming back the lost son hides the immense sorrow that has gone before. The finding has the losing in the background, the returning has the leaving under its cloak. Looking at the tender and joy-filled return, I have to dare to taste the sorrowful events that preceded it. Only when I have the courage to explore in depth what it means to leave home, can I come to a true understanding of the return. The soft yellow-brown of the son's underclothes looks beautiful when seen in rich harmony with the red of the father's cloak, but the truth of the matter is that the son is dressed in rags that betray the great misery that lies behind him. In the context of a compassionate embrace, our brokenness may appear beautiful, but our brokenness has no other beauty but the beauty that comes from the compassion that surrounds it.

To understand deeply the mystery of compassion, I have to look honestly at the reality that evokes it. The fact is that, long before turning and returning, the son left. He said to his father, "Let me have the share of the estate that will come to me," then he got together everything he had received and left. The evangelist Luke tells it all so simply and so matter-of-factly that it is difficult to realize fully that what is happening here is an unheard-of event: hurtful, offensive, and in radical contradiction to the most venerated tradition of the time. Kenneth Bailey, in his penetrating explanation of Luke's story, shows that the son's manner of leaving is tantamount to wishing his father dead. Bailey writes:

> For over fifteen years I have been asking people of all walks of life from Morocco to India and from Turkey to the Sudan about the implications of a son's request for his inheritance while the father is still living. The answer has always been emphatically the same . . . the conversation runs as follows:
> Has anyone ever made such a request in your village?
> Never!
> Could anyone ever make such a request?
> Impossible!
> If anyone ever did, what would happen?
> His father would beat him, of course!
> Why?
> The request means—he wants his father to die.

Bailey explains that the son asks not only for the division of the inheritance, but also for the right to dispose of his part. "After signing over his possessions to his son, the father still has the right to live off the proceeds . . . as long as he is alive. Here the younger son gets, and thus is assumed to have demanded, disposition to which, even more explicitly, he has no right until the death of his father. The implication of 'Father, I cannot wait for you to die' underlies both requests."

The son's "leaving" is, therefore, a much more offensive act than it seems at first reading. It is a heartless rejection of the home in which the son was born and nurtured and a break with the most precious tradition carefully upheld by the larger community of which he was a part. When Luke writes, "and left for a distant country," he indicates much more than the desire of a young man to see more of the world. He speaks about a drastic cutting loose from the way of living, thinking, and acting that has been handed down to him from generation to generation as a sacred legacy. More than disrespect, it is a betrayal of the treasured values of family and community. The "distant country" is the world in which everything considered holy at home is disregarded.

This explanation is significant to me, not only because it provides me with an accurate understanding of the parable in its historical context, but also—and most of all—because it summons me to recognize the younger son in myself. At first it seemed hard to discover in my own life's journey such a defiant rebellion. Rejecting the values of my own heritage is not part of the way I think of myself. But when I look carefully at the many more or less subtle ways I have preferred the distant country to the home close by, the younger son quickly emerges. I am speaking here about a spiritual "leaving home"—as quite distinct from the mere physical fact that I have spent most of my years outside my beloved Holland.

More than any other story in the Gospel, the parable of the prodigal son expresses the boundlessness of God's compassionate love. And when I place myself in that story under the light of that divine love, it becomes painfully clear that leaving home is much closer to my spiritual experience than I might have thought.

Rembrandt's painting of the father welcoming his son displays scarcely any external movement. In contrast to his 1636 etching of the prodigal son—full of action, the father running to the son and the son throwing himself at his father's feet—the Hermitage painting, made about thirty years later, is one of utter stillness. The father's touching the son is an everlasting blessing; the son resting against his father's breast is an eternal peace. Christian Tümpel writes: "The moment of receiving and forgiving in the stillness of its composition lasts without end. The movement of the father and the son speaks of something that passes not, but lasts forever." Jakob Rosenberg summarizes this vision beautifully when he writes: "The group of father and son is outwardly almost motionless, but inwardly all the more moved . . . the story deals not with the human love of an earthly father . . . what is meant and represented here is the divine love and mercy in its power to transform death into life."

Deaf to the Voice of Love

Leaving home is, then, much more than an historical event bound to time and place. It is a denial of the spiritual reality that I belong to God with every part of my being, that God holds me safe in an eternal embrace, that I am indeed carved in the palms of God's hands and hidden in their shadows. Leaving home means ignoring the truth that God has "fashioned me in secret, moulded me in the depths of the earth and knitted me together in my mother's womb." Leaving home is living as though I do not yet have a home and must look far and wide to find one.

Home is the center of my being where I can hear the voice that says: "You are my Beloved, on you my favor rests"—the same voice that gave life to the first Adam and spoke to Jesus, the second Adam; the same voice that speaks to all the children of God and sets them free to live in the midst of a dark world while remaining in the light.

I have heard that voice. It has spoken to me in the past and continues to speak to me now. It is the never-interrupted voice of love speaking from eternity and giving life and love whenever it is heard. When I hear that voice, I know that I am home with God and have nothing to fear. As the Beloved of my heavenly Father, "I can walk in the valley of darkness: no evil would I fear." As the Beloved, I can "cure the sick, raise the dead, cleanse the lepers, cast out devils." Having "received without charge," I can "give without charge." As the Beloved, I can confront, console, admonish, and encourage without fear of rejection or need for affirmation. As the Beloved, I can suffer persecution without desire for revenge and receive praise without using it as a proof of my goodness. As the Beloved, I can be tortured and killed without ever having to doubt that the love that is given to me is stronger than death. As the Beloved, I am free to live and give life, free also to die while giving life.

Jesus has made it clear to me that the same voice that he heard at the River Jordan and on Mount Tabor can also be heard by me. He has made it clear to me that just as he has his home with the Father, so do I. Praying to his Father for his disciples, he says: "They do not belong to the world, any more than I belong to the world. Consecrate them [set them aside] in the truth. As you sent me into the world, I have sent them into the world, and for their sake I consecrate myself so that they too may be consecrated in truth." These words reveal my true dwelling place, my true abode, my true home. Faith is the radical trust that home has always been there and always will be there. The somewhat stiff hands of the father rest on the prodigal's shoulders with the everlasting divine blessing: "You are my Beloved, on you my favor rests."

Yet over and over again I have left home. I have fled the hands of blessing and run off to faraway places searching for love! This is the great tragedy of my life and of the lives of so many I meet on my journey. Somehow I have become deaf to the voice that calls me the Beloved, have left the only place where I can hear that voice, and have gone off desperately hoping that I would find somewhere else what I could no longer find at home.

At first this sounds simply unbelievable. Why should I leave the place where all I need to hear can be heard? The more I think about this question, the more I realize that the true voice of love is a very soft and gentle voice speaking to me in the most hidden places of my being. It is not a boisterous voice, forcing itself on me and demanding attention. It is the voice of a nearly blind father who has cried much and died many deaths. It is a voice that can only be heard by those who allow themselves to be touched.

Sensing the touch of God's blessing hands and hearing the voice calling me the Beloved are one and the same. This became clear to the prophet Elijah. Elijah was standing on the mountain to meet God. First there came a hurricane, but God was not in the hurricane. Then there came an earthquake, but God was not in the earthquake. Then followed a fire, but God was not there either. Finally there came something very tender, called by some a soft breeze and by others a small voice. When Elijah sensed this, he covered his face because he knew that God was present. In the tenderness of God, voice was touch and touch was voice.

But there are many other voices, voices that are loud, full of promises and very seductive. These voices say, "Go out and prove that you are worth something." Soon after Jesus had heard the voice calling him the Beloved, he was led to the desert to hear those other voices. They told him to prove that he was worth love in being successful, popular, and powerful. Those same voices are not unfamiliar to me. They are always there and, always, they reach into those inner places where I question my own goodness and doubt my self-worth. They suggest that I am not going to be loved without my having earned it through determined efforts and hard work. They want me to prove to myself and others that I am worth being loved, and they keep pushing me to do everything possible to gain acceptance. They deny loudly that love is a totally free gift. I leave home every time I lose faith in the voice that calls me the Beloved and follow the voices that offer a great variety of ways to win the love I so much desire.

Almost from the moment I had ears to hear, I heard those

voices, and they have stayed with me ever since. They have come to me through my parents, my friends, my teachers, and my colleagues, but, most of all, they have come and still come through the mass media that surround me. And they say: "Show me that you are a good boy. You had better be better than your friend! How are your grades? Be sure you can make it through school! I sure hope you are going to make it on your own! What are your connections? Are you sure you want to be friends with those people? These trophies certainly show how good a player you were! Don't show your weakness, you'll be used! Have you made all the arrangements for your old age? When you stop being productive, people lose interest in you! When you are dead, you are dead!"

As long as I remain in touch with the voice that calls me the Beloved, these questions and counsels are quite harmless. Parents, friends, and teachers, even those who speak to me through the media, are mostly very sincere in their concerns. Their warnings and advice are well intended. In fact, they can be limited human expressions of an unlimited divine love. But when I forget that voice of the first unconditional love, then these innocent suggestions can easily start dominating my life and pull me into the "distant country." It is not very hard for me to know when this is happening. Anger, resentment, jealousy, desire for revenge, lust, greed, antagonisms, and rivalries are the obvious signs that I have left home. And that happens quite easily. When I pay careful attention to what goes on in my mind from moment to moment, I come to the disconcerting discovery that there are very few moments during my day when I am really free from these dark emotions, passions, and feelings.

Constantly falling back into an old trap, before I am even fully aware of it, I find myself wondering why someone hurt me, rejected me, or didn't pay attention to me. Without realizing it, I find myself brooding about someone else's success, my own loneliness, and the way the world abuses me. Despite my conscious intentions, I often catch myself daydreaming about becoming rich, powerful, and very famous. All of these mental games reveal to me the fragility of my faith that I am the Beloved One on whom God's favor rests. I am so afraid of being disliked, blamed, put aside, passed over, ignored, persecuted, and killed, that I am constantly developing strategies to defend myself and thereby assure myself of the love I think I need and deserve. And in so doing I move far away from my father's home and choose to dwell in a "distant country."

Searching Where It Cannot Be Found

At issue here is the question: "To whom do I belong? To God or to the world?" Many of my daily preoccupations suggest that I belong more to the world than to God. A little criticism makes me angry, and a little rejection makes me depressed. A little praise raises my spirits, and a little success excites me. It takes very little to raise me up or thrust me down. Often I am like a small boat on the ocean, completely at the mercy of its waves. All the time and energy I spend in keeping some kind of balance and preventing myself from being tipped over and drowning shows that my life is mostly a struggle for survival: not a holy struggle, but an anxious struggle resulting from the mistaken idea that it is the world that defines me.

As long as I keep running about asking: "Do you love me? Do you really love me?" I give all power to the voices of the world and put myself in bondage because the world is filled with "ifs." The world says: "Yes, I love you *if* you are good-looking, intelligent, and wealthy. I love you *if* you have a good education, a good job, and good connections. I love you *if* you produce much, sell much, and buy much." There are endless "ifs" hidden in the world's love. These "ifs" enslave me, since it is impossible to respond adequately to all of them. The world's love is and always will be conditional. As long as I keep looking for my true self in the world of conditional love, I will remain "hooked" to the world—trying, failing, and trying again. It is a world that fosters addictions because what it offers cannot satisfy the deepest craving of my heart.

"Addiction" might be the best word to explain the lostness that so deeply permeates contemporary society. Our addictions make us cling to what the world proclaims as the keys to self-fulfillment: accumulation of wealth and power; attainment of status and admiration; lavish consumption of food and drink, and sexual gratification without distinguishing between lust and love. These addictions create expectations that cannot but fail to satisfy our deepest needs. As long as we live within the world's delusions, our addictions condemn us to futile quests in "the distant country," leaving us to face an endless series of disillusionments while our sense of self remains unfulfilled. In these days of increasing addictions, we have wandered far away from our Father's home. The addicted life can aptly be designated a life lived in "a distant country." It is from there that our cry for deliverance rises up.

I am the prodigal son every time I search for unconditional love where it cannot be found. Why do I keep ignoring the place of true love and persist in looking for it elsewhere? Why do I keep leaving home where I am called a child of God, the Beloved of my Father? I am constantly surprised at how I keep taking the gifts God has given me—my health, my intellectual and emotional gifts—and keep using them to impress people, receive affirmation and praise, and compete for rewards, instead of developing them for the glory of God. Yes, I often carry them off to a "distant country" and put them in the service of an exploiting world that does not know their true value. It's almost as if I want to prove to myself and to my world that I do not need God's love, that I can make a life on my own, that I want to be fully independent. Beneath it all is the great rebellion, the radical "No" to the Father's love, the unspoken curse: "I wish you were dead." The prodigal son's "No" reflects Adam's original rebellion: his rejection of the God in whose love we are created and by whose love we are sustained. It is the rebellion that places me outside the garden, out of reach of the tree of life. It is the rebellion that makes me dissipate myself in a "distant country."

Looking again at Rembrandt's portrayal of the return of the younger son, I now see how much more is taking place than a mere compassionate gesture toward a wayward child. The great event I see is the end of the great rebellion. The rebellion of Adam and all his descendants is forgiven, and the original blessing by which Adam received everlasting life is restored. It seems to me now that these hands have always been stretched out—even when there were no shoulders upon which to rest them. God has never pulled back his arms, never withheld his blessing, never stopped considering his son the Beloved One. But the Father couldn't compel his son to stay home. He couldn't force his love on the Beloved. He had to let him go in freedom, even though he knew the pain it would cause both his son and himself. It was love itself that prevented him from keeping his son home at all cost. It was love itself that allowed him to let his son find his own life, even with the risk of losing it.

Here the mystery of my life is unveiled. I am loved so much that I am left free to leave home. The blessing is there from the beginning. I have left it and keep on leaving it. But the Father is always looking for me with outstretched arms to receive me back and whisper again in my ear: "You are my Beloved, on you my favor rests."

3

.

THE
YOUNGER SON'S
RETURN

*He squandered his money on a life of debauchery. When he had
spent it all, that country experienced a severe famine, and now he
began to feel the pinch; so he hired himself out to one of the local
inhabitants who put him on his farm to feed the pigs. And he
would willingly have filled himself with the husks the pigs were
eating, but no one would let him have them. Then he came to his
senses and said, "How many of my father's hired men have all
the food they want and more, and here am I dying of hunger! I
will leave this place and go to my father and say: Father, I have
sinned against heaven and against you; I no longer deserve to be
called your son; treat me as one of your hired men." So he left the
place and went back to his father.*

Being Lost

The young man held and blessed by the father is a poor, a very poor,
man. He left home with much pride and money, determined to live

his own life far away from his father and his community. He returns with nothing: his money, his health, his honor, his self-respect, his reputation . . . everything has been squandered.

Rembrandt leaves little doubt about his condition. His head is shaven. No longer the long curly hair with which Rembrandt had painted himself as the proud, defiant prodigal son in the brothel. The head is that of a prisoner whose name has been replaced by a number. When a man's hair is shaved off, whether in prison or in the army, in a hazing ritual or in a concentration camp, he is robbed of one of the marks of his individuality. The clothes Rembrandt gives him are underclothes, barely covering his emaciated body. The father and the tall man observing the scene wear wide red cloaks, giving them status and dignity. The kneeling son has no cloak. The yellow-brown, torn undergarment just covers his exhausted, worn-out body from which all strength is gone. The soles of his feet tell the story of a long and humiliating journey. The left foot, slipped out of its worn sandal, is scarred. The right foot, only partially covered by a broken sandal, also speaks of suffering and misery. This is a man dispossessed of everything . . . except for one thing, his sword. The only remaining sign of dignity is the short sword hanging from his hips—the badge of his nobility. Even in the midst of his debasement, he had clung to the truth that he still was the son of his father. Otherwise, he would have sold his so valuable sword, the symbol of his sonship. The sword is there to show me that, although he came back speaking as a beggar and an outcast, he had not forgotten that he still was the son of his father. It was this remembered and valued sonship that finally persuaded him to turn back.

I see before me a man who went deep into a foreign land and lost everything he took with him. I see emptiness, humiliation, and defeat. He who was so much like his father now looks worse than his father's servants. He has become like a slave.

What happened to the son in the distant country? Aside from all the material and physical consequences, what were the inner consequences of the son's leaving home? The sequence of events is quite predictable. The farther I run away from the place where God dwells, the less I am able to hear the voice that calls me the Beloved, and the less I hear that voice, the more entangled I become in the manipulations and power games of the world.

It goes somewhat like this: I am not so sure anymore that I have a safe home, and I observe other people who seem to be better off than I. I wonder how I can get to where they are. I try hard to please, to achieve success, to be recognized. When I fail, I feel jealous or resentful of these others. When I succeed, I worry that others will be jealous or resentful of me. I become suspicious or defensive and increasingly afraid that I won't get what I so much desire or will lose what I already have. Caught in this tangle of needs and wants, I no longer know my own motivations. I feel victimized by my surroundings and distrustful of what others are doing or saying. Always on my guard, I lose my inner freedom and start dividing the world into those who are for me and those who are against me. I wonder if anyone really cares. I start looking for validations of my distrust. And wherever I go, I see them, and I say: "No one can be trusted." And then I wonder whether *anyone* ever really loved me. The world around me becomes dark. My heart grows heavy. My body is filled with sorrows. My life loses meaning. I have become a lost soul.

The younger son became fully aware of how lost he was when no one in his surroundings showed the slightest interest in him. They noticed him only as long as he could be used for their purposes. But when he had no money left to spend and no gifts left to give, he stopped existing for them. It is hard for me to imagine what it means to be a complete foreigner, a person to whom no one shows any sign of recognition. Real loneliness comes when we have lost all sense of having things in common. When no one wanted to give him the food he was giving to the pigs, the younger son realized that he wasn't even considered a fellow human being. I am only partially aware of how much I rely on some degree of acceptance. Common background, history, vision, religion, and education; common relationships, life-styles, and customs; common age and profession; all of these can serve as bases for acceptance. Whenever I meet a new person, I always look for something we have in common. That seems a normal, spontaneous reaction. When I say, "I am from Holland," the response is often: "Oh, I have been there," or "I have a friend there," or "Oh, windmills, tulips, and wooden shoes!"

Whatever the reaction, there is always a mutual search for a common link. The less we have in common, the harder it is to be together and the more estranged we feel. When I know neither the language nor the customs of others, when I do not understand their life-style or religion, their rituals or their art, when I do not know their food and manner of eating . . . then I feel even more foreign and lost.

When the younger son was no longer considered a human being by the people around him, he felt the profundity of his isolation, the deepest loneliness one can experience. He was truly lost, and it was this complete lostness that brought him to his senses. He was shocked into the awareness of his utter alienation and suddenly understood that he had embarked on the road to death. He had become so disconnected from what gives life—family, friends, community, acquaintances, and even food—that he realized that death would be the natural next step. All at once he saw clearly the path he had chosen and where it would lead him; he understood his own death choice; and he knew that one more step in the direction he was going would take him to self-destruction.

In that critical moment, what was it that allowed him to opt for life? It was the rediscovery of his deepest self.

Claiming Childhood

Whatever he had lost, be it his money, his friends, his reputation, his self-respect, his inner joy and peace—one or all—he still remained his father's child. And so he says to himself: "How many of my father's hired men have all the food they want and more, and here am I dying of hunger! I will leave this place and go to my father and say: Father, I have sinned against heaven and against you; I no longer deserve to be called your son; treat me as one of your hired men."

With these words in his heart, he was able to turn, to leave the foreign country, and go home.

The meaning of the younger son's return is succinctly expressed in the words: "Father, . . . I no longer deserve to be called your son." On the one hand the younger son realizes that he has lost the dignity of his sonship, but at the same time that sense of lost dignity makes him also aware that he is indeed the *son* who had dignity to lose.

The younger son's return takes place in the very moment that he reclaims his sonship, even though he has lost all the dignity that belongs to it. In fact, it was the loss of everything that brought him to the bottom line of his identity. He hit the bedrock of his sonship. In retrospect, it seems that the prodigal had to lose everything to come into touch with the ground of his being. When he found himself desiring to be treated as one of the pigs, he realized that he was not a pig but a human being, a son of his father. This realization became the basis for his choice to live instead of to die. Once he had come again in touch with the truth of his sonship, he could hear—although faintly—the voice calling him the Beloved and feel—although distantly—the touch of blessing. This awareness of and confidence in his father's love, misty as it may have been, gave him the strength to claim for himself his sonship, even though that claim could not be based on any merit.

A few years ago, I, myself, was very concretely confronted with the choice: to return or not to return. A friendship that at first seemed promising and life-giving gradually pulled me farther and farther away from home until I finally found myself completely obsessed by it. In a spiritual sense, I found myself squandering all I had been given by my father to keep the friendship alive. I couldn't pray any longer. I had lost interest in my work and found it increasingly hard to pay attention to other people's concerns. As much as I realized how self-destructive my thoughts and actions were, I kept being drawn by my love-hungry heart to deceptive ways of gaining a sense of self-worth.

Then, when finally the friendship broke down completely, I

had to choose between destroying myself or trusting that the love I was looking for did, in fact, exist . . . back home! A voice, weak as it seemed, whispered that no human being would ever be able to give me the love I craved, that no friendship, no intimate relationship, no community would ever be able to satisfy the deepest needs of my wayward heart. That soft but persistent voice spoke to me about my vocation, my early commitments, the many gifts I had received in my father's house. That voice called me "son."

The anguish of abandonment was so biting that it was hard, almost impossible, to believe that voice. But friends, seeing my despair, kept urging me to step over my anguish and to trust that there was someone waiting for me at home. Finally, I chose for containment instead of more dissipation and went to a place where I could be alone. There, in my solitude, I started to walk home slowly and hesitantly, hearing ever more clearly the voice that says: "You are my Beloved, on you my favor rests."

This painful, yet hopeful, experience brought me to the core of the spiritual struggle for the right choice. God says: "I am offering you life or death, blessing or curse. Choose life, then, so that you . . . may live in the love of Yahweh your God, obeying his voice, holding fast to him." Indeed, it is a question of life or death. Do we accept the rejection of the world that imprisons us, or do we claim the freedom of the children of God? *We* must choose.

Judas betrayed Jesus. Peter denied him. Both were lost children. Judas, no longer able to hold on to the truth that he remained God's child, hung himself. In terms of the prodigal son, he sold the sword of his sonship. Peter, in the midst of his despair, claimed it and returned with many tears. Judas chose death. Peter chose life. I realize that this choice is always before me. Constantly I am tempted to wallow in my own lostness and lose touch with my original goodness, my God-given humanity, my basic blessedness, and thus allow the powers of death to take charge. This happens over and over again whenever I say to myself: "I am no good. I am useless. I am worthless. I am unlovable. I am a nobody." There are always countless events and situations that I can single out to convince myself and others that my life is just not worth living, that I am only a burden, a problem, a source of conflict, or an exploiter of other people's time and energy. Many people live with this dark, inner sense of themselves. In contrast to the prodigal, they let the darkness absorb them so completely that there is no light left to turn toward and return to. They might not kill themselves physically, but spiritually they are no longer alive. They have given up faith in their original goodness and, thus, also in their Father who has given them their humanity.

But when God created man and woman in his own image, he saw that "it was very good," and, despite the dark voices, no man or woman can ever change that.

The choice for my own sonship, however, is not an easy one. The dark voices of my surrounding world try to persuade me that I am no good and that I can only become good by earning my goodness through "making it" up the ladder of success. These voices lead me quickly to forget the voice that calls me "my son, the Beloved," reminding me of my being loved independently of any acclaim or accomplishment. These dark voices drown out that gentle, soft, light-giving voice that keeps calling me "my favorite one"; they drag me to the periphery of my existence and make me doubt that there is a loving God waiting for me at the very center of my being.

But leaving the foreign country is only the beginning. The way home is long and arduous. What to do on the way back to the Father? It is very clear what the prodigal son does. He prepares a scenario. As he turned, remembering his sonship, he said to himself: "I will leave this place and go to my father and say: Father, I have sinned against heaven and against you; I no longer deserve to be called your son; treat me as one of your hired men." As I read these words, I am keenly aware of how full my inner life is with this kind of talk. In fact, I am seldom without some imaginary encounter in my head in which I explain myself, boast or apologize, proclaim or defend, evoke praise or pity. It seems that I am perpetually involved in long dialogues with absent partners, anticipating their questions and preparing my responses. I am amazed by the emotional energy that goes into these inner ruminations and murmurings. Yes, I *am* leaving the foreign country. Yes, I *am* going home . . . but why all this preparation of speeches which will never be delivered?

The reason is clear. Although claiming my true identity as a child of God, I still live as though the God to whom I am returning demands an explanation. I still think about his love as conditional and about home as a place I am not yet fully sure of. While walking home, I keep entertaining doubts about whether I will be truly welcome when I get there. As I look at my spiritual journey, my long and fatiguing trip home, I see how full it is of guilt about the past and worries about the future. I realize my failures and know that I have lost the dignity of my sonship, but I am not yet able to fully believe that where my failings are great, "grace is always greater." Still clinging to my sense of worthlessness, I project for myself a place far below that which belongs to the son. Belief in total, absolute forgiveness does not come readily. My human experience tells me that forgiveness boils down to the willingness of the other to forgo revenge and to show me some measure of charity.

The Long Way Home

The prodigal's return is full of ambiguities. He is traveling in the right direction, but what confusion! He admits that he was unable to make it on his own and confesses that he would get better treatment as a slave in his father's home than as an outcast in a foreign land, but he is still far from trusting his father's love. He knows that he is still the son, but tells himself that he has lost the dignity to be called "son," and he prepares himself to accept the status of a "hired man" so that he will at least survive. There is repentance, but not a repentance in the light of the immense love of a forgiving God. It is a self-serving repentance that offers the possibility of survival. I know this state of mind and heart quite well. It is like saying: "Well, I couldn't make it on my own, I have to acknowledge that God is the only resource left to me. I will go to God and ask for forgiveness in the hope that I will receive a minimal punishment and be allowed to survive on the condition of hard labor." God remains a harsh, judg-mental God. It is this God who makes me feel guilty and worried and calls up in me all these self-serving apologies. Submission to this God does not create true inner freedom, but breeds only bitterness and resentment.

One of the greatest challenges of the spiritual life is to receive God's forgiveness. There is something in us humans that keeps us clinging to our sins and prevents us from letting God erase our past and offer us a completely new beginning. Sometimes it even seems as though I want to prove to God that my darkness is too great to overcome. While God wants to restore me to the full dignity of sonship, I keep insisting that I will settle for being a hired servant. But do I truly want to be restored to the full responsibility of the son? Do I truly want to be so totally forgiven that a completely new way of living becomes possible? Do I trust myself and such a radical reclamation? Do I want to break away from my deep-rooted rebel-lion against God and surrender myself so absolutely to God's love that a new person can emerge? Receiving forgiveness requires a total willingness to let God be God and do all the healing, restoring, and renewing. As long as I want to do even a part of that myself, I end up with partial solutions, such as becoming a hired servant. As a hired servant, I can still keep my distance, still revolt, reject, strike, run away, or complain about my pay. As the beloved son, I have to claim my full dignity and begin preparing myself to become the father.

It is clear that the distance between the turning around and the arrival at home needs to be traveled wisely and with discipline. The discipline is that of becoming a child of God. Jesus makes it clear that the way to God is the same as the way to a new childhood. "Unless you turn and become like little children you will never enter the Kingdom of Heaven." Jesus does not ask me to remain a child but to become one. Becoming a child is living toward a second innocence: not the innocence of the newborn infant, but the innocence that is reached through conscious choices.

How can those who have come to this second childhood, this

second innocence, be described? Jesus does this very clearly in the Beatitudes. Shortly after hearing the voice calling him the Beloved, and soon after rejecting Satan's voice daring him to prove to the world that he is worth being loved, he begins his public ministry. One of his first steps is to call disciples to follow him and share in his ministry. Then Jesus goes up onto the mountain, gathers his disciples around him, and says: "How blessed are the poor, the gentle, those who mourn, those who hunger and thirst for uprightness, the merciful, the pure of heart, the peacemakers, and those who are persecuted in the cause of uprightness."

These words present a portrait of the child of God. It is a self-portrait of Jesus, the Beloved Son. It is also a portrait of me as I must be. The Beatitudes offer me the simplest route for the journey home, back into the house of my Father. And along this route I will discover the joys of the second childhood: comfort, mercy, and an ever clearer vision of God. And as I reach home and feel the embrace of my Father, I will realize that not only heaven will be mine to claim, but that the earth as well will become my inheritance, a place where I can live in freedom without obsessions and compulsions.

Becoming a child is living the Beatitudes and so finding the narrow gate into the Kingdom. Did Rembrandt know about this? I don't know whether the parable leads me to see new aspects of his painting, or whether his painting leads me to discover new aspects of the parable. But looking at the head of the boy-come-home, I can see the second childhood portrayed.

I vividly remember showing the Rembrandt painting to friends and asking them what they saw. One of them, a young woman, stood up, walked to the large print of the *Prodigal Son,* and put her hand on the head of the younger son. Then she said, "This is the head of a baby who just came out of his mother's womb. Look, it is still wet, and the face is still fetus-like." All of us who were present saw suddenly what she saw. Was Rembrandt portraying not simply the return to the Father, but also the return to the womb of God who is Mother as well as Father?

Until then I had thought of the shaved head of the boy as the head of someone who had been a prisoner, or lived in a concentration camp. I had thought of his face as the emaciated face of an ill-treated hostage. And that may still be all that Rembrandt wanted to show. But since that meeting with my friends, it is no longer possible for me to look at his painting without seeing there a little baby re-entering the mother's womb. This helps me to understand more clearly the road I am to walk on my way home.

Isn't the little child poor, gentle, and pure of heart? Isn't the little child weeping in response to every little pain? Isn't the little child the peacemaker hungry and thirsty for uprightness and the final victim of persecution? And what of Jesus himself, the Word of God who became flesh, dwelt for nine months in Mary's womb, and came into this world as a little child worshipped by shepherds from close by and by wise men from far away? The eternal Son became a child so that I might become a child again and so re-enter with him into the Kingdom of the Father. "In all truth I tell you," Jesus said to Nicodemus, "no one can see the Kingdom of God without being born from above."

The True Prodigal

I am touching here the mystery that Jesus himself became the prodigal son for our sake. He left the house of his heavenly Father, came to a foreign country, gave away all that he had, and returned through his cross to his Father's home. All of this he did, not as a rebellious son, but as the obedient son, sent out to bring home all the lost children of God. Jesus, who told the story to those who criticized him for associating with sinners, himself lived the long and painful journey that he describes.

When I began to reflect on the parable and Rembrandt's portrayal of it, I never thought of the exhausted young man with the face of a newborn baby as Jesus. But now, after so many hours of intimate contemplation, I feel blessed by this vision. Isn't the broken young man kneeling before his father the "lamb of God that takes away the sin of the world"? Isn't he the innocent one who became sin for us? Isn't he the one who didn't "cling to his equality with God," but "became as human beings are"? Isn't he the sinless Son of God who cried out on the cross: "My God, my God, why have you forsaken me?" Jesus is the prodigal son of the prodigal Father who gave away everything the Father had entrusted to him so that I could become like him and return with him to his Father's home.

Seeing Jesus himself as the prodigal son goes far beyond the traditional interpretation of the parable. Nonetheless, this vision holds a great secret. I am gradually discovering what it means to say that my sonship and the sonship of Jesus are one, that my return and the return of Jesus are one, that my home and the home of Jesus are one. There is no journey to God outside of the journey that Jesus made. The one who told the story of the prodigal son is the Word of God, "through whom all things came into being." He "became flesh, lived among us," and made us part of his fullness.

Once I look at the story of the prodigal son with the eyes of faith, the "return" of the prodigal becomes the return of the Son of God who has drawn all people into himself and brings them home to his heavenly Father. As Paul says: "God wanted all fullness to be found in him and through him to reconcile all things to him, everything in heaven and everything on earth."

Frère Pierre Marie, the founder of the Fraternity of Jerusalem, a community of monks living in the city, reflects on Jesus as the prodigal son in a very poetic and biblical way. He writes:

> He, who is born not from human stock, or human desire or human will, but from God himself, one day took to himself everything that was under his footstool and he left with his inheritance, his title of Son, and the whole ransom price. He left for a far country . . . the faraway land . . . where he became as human beings are and emptied himself. His own people did not accept him and his first bed was a bed of straw! Like a root in arid ground, he grew up before us, he was despised, the lowest of men, before

whom one covers his face. Very soon, he came to know exile, hostility, loneliness . . . After having given away everything in a life of bounty, his worth, his peace, his light, his truth, his life . . . all the treasures of knowledge and wisdom and the hidden mystery kept secret for endless ages; after having lost himself among the lost children of the house of Israel, spending his time with the sick (and not with the well-to-do), with the sinners (and not with the just), and even with the prostitutes to whom he promised entrance into the Kingdom of his Father; after having been treated as a glutton and a drunkard, as a friend of tax collectors and sinners, as a Samaritan, a possessed, a blasphemer; after having offered everything, even his body and his blood; after having felt deeply in himself sadness, anguish, and a troubled soul; after having gone to the bottom of despair, with which he voluntarily dressed himself as being abandoned by his Father far away from the source of living water, he cried out from the cross on which he was nailed: "I am thirsty." He was laid to rest in the dust and the shadow of death. And there, on the third day, he rose up from the depths of hell to where he had descended, burdened with the crimes of us all, he bore our sins, our sorrows he carried. Standing straight, he cried out: "Yes, I am ascending to my Father, and your Father, to my God, and your God." And he reascended to heaven. Then in the silence, looking at his Son and all his children, since his Son had become all in all, the Father said to his servants, "Quick! Bring out the best robe and put it on him; put a ring on his finger and sandals on his feet; let us eat and celebrate! Because my children who, as you know, were dead have returned to life; they were lost and have been found again! My prodigal Son has brought them all back." They all began to have a feast dressed in their long robes, washed white in the blood of the Lamb.

Looking again at Rembrandt's *Prodigal Son,* I see him now in a new way. I see him as Jesus returning to his Father and my Father, his God and my God.

It is unlikely that Rembrandt himself ever thought of the prodigal son in this way. This understanding was not a customary part of the preaching and writing of his time. Nevertheless, to see in this tired, broken young man the person of Jesus himself brings much comfort and consolation. The young man being embraced by the Father is no longer just one repentant sinner, but the whole of humanity returning to God. The broken body of the prodigal becomes the broken body of humanity, and the baby-like face of the returning child becomes the face of all suffering people longing to reenter the lost paradise. Thus Rembrandt's painting becomes more than the mere portrayal of a moving parable. It becomes the summary of the history of our salvation. The light surrounding both Father and Son now speaks of the glory that awaits the children of God. It calls to mind the majestic words of John: ". . . we are already God's children, but what we shall be in the future has not yet been revealed. We are well aware that when he appears we shall be like him, because we shall see him as he really is."

But neither Rembrandt's painting nor the parable it depicts leaves us in a state of ecstasy. When I saw the central scene of the father embracing his returning son on the poster in Simone's office, I was not yet aware of the four bystanders watching the scene. But now I know the faces of those surrounding the "return." They are enigmatic to say the least, especially that of the tall man standing at the right side of the painting. Yes, there is beauty, glory, salvation . . . but there are also the critical eyes of uncommitted onlookers. They add a restraining note to the painting and prevent any notions of a quick, romantic solution to the question of spiritual reconciliation. The journey of the younger son cannot be separated from that of his elder brother. And so it is to him that I now—with some temerity—turn my attention.

Part II

·

THE

ELDER
SON

Now the elder son was out in the fields, and on his way back, as he drew near the house, he could hear music and dancing. Calling one of the servants he asked what it was all about. The servant told him, "Your brother has come, and your father has killed the calf we had been fattening because he has got him back safe and sound." He was angry then and refused to go in, and his father came out and began to urge him to come in; but he retorted to his father, "All these years I have slaved for you and never once disobeyed any orders of yours, yet you never offered me so much as a kid for me to celebrate with my friends. But, for this son of yours, when he comes back after swallowing up your property —he and his loose women—you kill the calf we had been fattening."

The father said, "My son, you are with me always, and all I have is yours. But it was only right we should celebrate and rejoice, because your brother here was dead and has come to life; he was lost and is found."

4

.

REMBRANDT
AND THE
ELDER SON

During my hours in the Hermitage, quietly looking at the *Prodigal Son,* I never for a moment questioned that the man standing at the right of the platform on which the father embraces his returned son was the elder son. The way he stands there looking at the great gesture of welcome leaves no room for doubt as to whom Rembrandt wanted to portray. I made many notes describing this stern-looking, distant observer and saw there everything Jesus tells us about the elder son.

Still, the parable makes it clear that the elder son is not yet home when the father embraces his lost son and shows him his mercy. To the contrary, the story shows that, when the elder son finally returns from his work, the welcome-home party for his brother is already in full swing.

I am surprised at how easily I missed the discrepancy between Rembrandt's painting and the parable, and simply took it for granted that Rembrandt wanted to paint both brothers in his portrayal of the prodigal son.

When I returned home and began to read all the historical studies of the painting, I quickly realized that many critics were much less sure than I as to the identity of the man standing at the right. Some described him as an old man, and some even questioned whether Rembrandt himself had painted him.

But then one day, more than a year after my visit to the Hermitage, a friend, Ivan Dyer, with whom I had often discussed my interest in the *Prodigal* painting, sent me a copy of Barbara Joan Haeger's "The Religious Significance of Rembrandt's Return of the Prodigal Son." This brilliant study, which puts the painting into the context of the visual and iconographic tradition of Rembrandt's time, brought the elder son back into the picture.

Haeger shows that, in the biblical commentaries and paintings of Rembrandt's time, the parable of the Pharisee and the tax collector and the parable of the prodigal son were closely linked. Rembrandt follows that tradition. The seated man beating his breast and looking at the returning son is a steward representing the sinners and tax collectors, while the standing man looking at the father in a somewhat enigmatic way is the elder son, representing the Pharisees and scribes. By putting the elder son in the painting as the most prominent witness, however, Rembrandt goes not only beyond the literal text of the parable, but also beyond the painting tradition of his time. Thus Rembrandt holds on, as Haeger says, "not to the letter but to the spirit of the biblical text."

Barbara Haeger's findings are much more than a happy affirmation of my earliest intuition. They help me to see *The Return of the Prodigal Son* as a work that summarizes the great spiritual battle and the great choices this battle demands. By painting not only the younger son in the arms of his father, but also the elder son who can still choose for or against the love that is offered to him, Rembrandt presents me with the "inner drama of the soul"—his as well as my own. Just as the parable of the prodigal son encapsulates the core message of the Gospel and calls the listeners to make their own choices in face of it, so, too, does Rembrandt's painting sum up his own spiritual struggle and invite his viewers to make a personal decision about their lives.

Thus Rembrandt's bystanders make his painting a work that engages the viewer in a very personal way. In the fall of 1983, when I first saw the poster showing the central part of the painting, I immediately felt that I was personally called to something. Now that I am better acquainted with the whole painting and especially with the meaning of the prominent witness on the right, I am more than ever convinced of what an enormous spiritual challenge this painting represents.

Looking at the younger son and reflecting on Rembrandt's life, it became quite apparent to me that Rembrandt must have understood him in a personal way. When he painted *The Return of the Prodigal Son,* he had lived a life marked by great self-confidence, success, and fame, followed by many painful losses, disappointments, and failures. Through it all he had moved from the exterior light to the interior light, from the portrayal of external events to the portrayal of the inner meanings, from a life full of things and people to a life more marked by solitude and silence. With age, he grew more interior and still. It was a spiritual homecoming.

But the elder son is also part of Rembrandt's life experience, and many modern biographers are, in fact, critical of the romantic vision of his life. They stress that Rembrandt was much more subject to the demands of his sponsors and his need for money than is generally believed, that his subjects are often more the result of the prevailing fashions of his time than of his spiritual vision, and that his failures have as much to do with his self-righteous and obnoxious character as with the lack of appreciation on the part of his milieu.

Different new biographies see in Rembrandt more a selfish,

calculating manipulator than a searcher for spiritual truth. They contend that many of his paintings, brilliant as they are, are much less spiritual than they seem. My initial reaction to these demythologizing studies of Rembrandt was one of shock. In particular, the biography by Gary Schwartz—which leaves little room for romanticizing Rembrandt—made me wonder if anything like a "conversion" had ever taken place. It is quite clear from the many recent studies of Rembrandt's relationships with his patrons, those who ordered and bought his work, as well as with family and friends, that he was a very difficult person to get along with. Schwartz describes him as a "bitter, revengeful person who used all permissible and impermissible weapons to attack those who came in his way."

Indeed, Rembrandt was known to act often selfishly, arrogantly, and even vengefully. This is most vividly shown in the way he treated Geertje Dircx, with whom he had been living for six years. He used Geertje's brother, who had been given the power of attorney by Geertje herself, to "collect testimony from neighbors against her, so that she could be sent away to an insane asylum." The outcome was Geertje's confinement in a mental institution. When the possibility later arose that she could be released, "Rembrandt hired an agent to collect evidence against her, to make certain that she stay locked up."

During the year 1649, when these tragic events began to happen, Rembrandt was so consumed by them that he produced no work. At this point another Rembrandt emerges, a man lost in bitterness and desire for revenge, and capable of betrayal.

This Rembrandt is hard to face. It is not so difficult to sympathize with a lustful character who indulges in the hedonistic pleasures of the world, then repents, returns home, and becomes a very spiritual person. But appreciating a man with deep resentments, wasting much of his precious time in rather petty court cases and constantly alienating people by his arrogant behavior, is much harder to do. Yet, to the best of my knowledge, that, too, was a part of his life, a part I cannot ignore.

Rembrandt is as much the elder son of the parable as he is the younger. When, during the last years of his life, he painted both sons in his *Return of the Prodigal Son,* he had lived a life in which neither the lostness of the younger son nor the lostness of the elder son was alien to him. Both needed healing and forgiveness. Both needed to come home. Both needed the embrace of a forgiving father. But from the story itself, as well as from Rembrandt's painting, it is clear that the hardest conversion to go through is the conversion of the one who stayed home.

5

.

THE

ELDER SON

LEAVES

Now the elder son was out in the fields, and on his way back, as he drew near the house, he could hear music and dancing. Calling one of the servants, he asked what it was all about. The servant told him, "Your brother has come, and your father has killed the calf we had been fattening because he has got him back safe and sound." He was angry then and refused to go in, and his father came out and began to urge him to come in; but he retorted to his father, "All these years I have slaved for you and never once disobeyed any orders of yours, yet you never offered me so much as a kid for me to celebrate with my friends. But, for this son of yours, when he comes back after swallowing up your property—he and his loose women—you kill the calf we had been fattening."

Standing with Clasped Hands

During the hours I spent in the Hermitage looking at Rembrandt's painting, I became increasingly fascinated by the figure of the elder son. I recall gazing at him for long periods and wondering what was going on in this man's mind and heart. He is, without any doubt, the main observer of the younger son's homecoming. At the time when I was familiar only with the detail of the painting in which the father embraces his returning son, it was rather easy to perceive it as inviting, moving, and reassuring. But when I saw the whole painting, I quickly realized the complexity of the reunion. The main observer, watching the father embracing his returning son, appears very withdrawn. He looks at the father, but not with joy. He does not reach out, nor does he smile or express welcome. He simply stands there—at the side of the platform—apparently not eager to come higher up.

It is true that the "return" is the central event of the painting; however, it is not situated at the physical center of the canvas. It takes place at the left side of the painting, while the tall, stern elder son dominates the right side. There is a large open space separating the father and his elder son, a space that creates a tension asking for resolution.

With the elder son in the painting, it is no longer possible for me to sentimentalize the "return." The main observer is keeping his distance, seemingly unwilling to participate in the father's welcome. What is going on inside this man? What will he do? Will he come closer and embrace his brother as his father did, or will he walk away in anger and disgust?

Ever since my friend Bart remarked that I may be much more like the elder brother than the younger, I have observed this "man at the right" with more attentiveness and have seen many new and hard things. The way in which the elder son has been painted by Rembrandt shows him to be very much like his father. Both are bearded and wear large red cloaks over their shoulders. These externals suggest that he and his father have much in common, and this commonality is underlined by the light on the elder son which connects his face in a very direct way with the luminous face of his father.

But what a painful difference between the two! The father bends over his returning son. The elder son stands stiffly erect, a posture accentuated by the long staff reaching from his hand to the floor. The father's mantle is wide and welcoming; the son's hangs flat over his body. The father's hands are spread out and touch the homecomer in a gesture of blessing; the son's are clasped together and held close to his chest. There is light on both faces, but the light from the father's face flows through his whole body—especially his hands—and engulfs the younger son in a great halo of luminous warmth; whereas the light on the face of the elder son is cold and constricted. His figure remains in the dark, and his clasped hands remain in the shadows.

The parable that Rembrandt painted might well be called "The Parable of the Lost Sons." Not only did the younger son, who left home to look for freedom and happiness in a distant country, get lost, but the one who stayed home also became a lost man. Exteriorly he did all the things a good son is supposed to do, but, interiorly, he wandered away from his father. He did his duty, worked hard every day, and fulfilled all his obligations but became increasingly unhappy and unfree.

Lost in Resentment

It is hard for me to concede that this bitter, resentful, angry man might be closer to me in a spiritual way than the lustful younger brother. Yet the more I think about the elder son, the more I recognize myself in him. As the eldest son in my own family, I know well what it feels like to have to be a model son.

I often wonder if it is not especially the elder sons who want to live up to the expectations of their parents and be considered obedient and dutiful. They often want to please. They often fear being a disappointment to their parents. But they often also experience, quite early in life, a certain envy toward their younger brothers and sisters, who seem to be less concerned about pleasing and much freer in "doing their own thing." For me, this was certainly the case. And all my life I have harbored a strange curiosity for the disobedient life that I myself didn't dare to live, but which I saw being lived by many around me. I did all the proper things, mostly complying with the agendas set by the many parental figures in my life—teachers, spiritual directors, bishops, and popes—but at the same time I often wondered why I didn't have the courage to "run away" as the younger son did.

It is strange to say this, but, deep in my heart, I have known the feeling of envy toward the wayward son. It is the emotion that arises when I see my friends having a good time doing all sorts of things that I condemn. I called their behavior reprehensible or even immoral, but at the same time I often wondered why I didn't have the nerve to do some of it or all of it myself.

The obedient and dutiful life of which I am proud or for which I am praised feels, sometimes, like a burden that was laid on my shoulders and continues to oppress me, even when I have accepted it to such a degree that I cannot throw it off. I have no difficulty identifying with the elder son of the parable who complained: "All these years I have slaved for you and never once disobeyed any orders of yours, yet you never offered me so much as a kid for me to celebrate with my friends." In this complaint, obedience and duty have become a burden, and service has become slavery.

All of this became very real for me when a friend who had recently become a Christian criticized me for not being very prayerful. His criticism made me very angry. I said to myself, "How dare he teach me a lesson about prayer! For years he has lived a carefree and undisciplined life, while I since childhood have scrupulously lived the life of faith. Now he is converted and starts telling me how to behave!" This inner resentment reveals to me my own "lostness." I had stayed home and didn't wander off, but I had not yet lived a free life in my father's house. My anger and envy showed me my own bondage.

This is not something unique to me. There are many elder sons and elder daughters who are lost while still at home. And it is this lostness—characterized by judgment and condemnation, anger and resentment, bitterness and jealousy—that is so pernicious and so damaging to the human heart. Often we think about lostness in terms of actions that are quite visible, even spectacular. The younger son sinned in a way we can easily identify. His lostness is quite obvious. He misused his money, his time, his friends, his own body. What he did was wrong; not only his family and friends knew it, but he himself as well. He rebelled against morality and allowed himself to be swept away by his own lust and greed. There is something very clear-cut about his misbehavior. Then, having seen that all his way-ward behavior led to nothing but misery, the younger son came to his senses, turned around, and asked for forgiveness. We have here a classical human failure, with a straightforward resolution. Quite easy to understand and sympathize with.

The lostness of the elder son, however, is much harder to iden-tify. After all, he did all the right things. He was obedient, dutiful, law-abiding, and hardworking. People respected him, admired him, praised him, and likely considered him a model son. Outwardly, the elder son was faultless. But when confronted by his father's joy at the return of his younger brother, a dark power erupts in him and boils to the surface. Suddenly, there becomes glaringly visible a resentful, proud, unkind, selfish person, one that had remained deeply hidden, even though it had been growing stronger and more powerful over the years.

Looking deeply into myself and then around me at the lives of other people, I wonder which does more damage, lust or resent-ment? There is so much resentment among the "just" and the "righ-teous." There is so much judgment, condemnation, and prejudice among the "saints." There is so much frozen anger among the peo-ple who are so concerned about avoiding "sin."

The lostness of the resentful "saint" is so hard to reach precisely because it is so closely wedded to the desire to be good and virtuous. I know, from my own life, how diligently I have tried to be good, acceptable, likable, and a worthy example for others. There was al-ways the conscious effort to avoid the pitfalls of sin and the constant fear of giving in to temptation. But with all of that there came a seriousness, a moralistic intensity—and even a touch of fanaticism—that made it increasingly difficult to feel at home in my Father's house. I became less free, less spontaneous, less playful, and others came to see me more and more as a somewhat "heavy" person.

Without Joy

When I listen carefully to the words with which the elder son attacks his father—self-righteous, self-pitying, jealous words—I hear a deeper complaint. It is the complaint that comes from a heart that feels it never received what it was due. It is the complaint expressed in countless subtle and not-so-subtle ways, forming a bedrock of human resentment. It is the complaint that cries out: "I tried so hard, worked so long, did so much, and still I have not received what others get so easily. Why do people not thank me, not invite me, not play with me, not honor me, while they pay so much attention to those who take life so easily and so casually?"

It is in this spoken or unspoken complaint that I recognize the elder son in me. Often I catch myself complaining about little rejections, little impolitenesses, little negligences. Time and again I discover within me that murmuring, whining, grumbling, lamenting, and griping that go on and on even against my will. The more I dwell on the matters in question, the worse my state becomes. The more I analyze it, the more reason I see for complaint. And the more deeply I enter it, the more complicated it gets. There is an enormous, dark drawing power to this inner complaint. Condemnation of others and self-condemnation, self-righteousness and self-rejection keep reinforcing each other in an ever more vicious way. Every time I allow myself to be seduced by it, it spins me down in an endless spiral of self-rejection. As I let myself be drawn into the vast interior labyrinth of my complaints, I become more and more lost until, in the end, I feel myself to be the most misunderstood, rejected, neglected, and despised person in the world.

Of one thing I am sure. Complaining is self-perpetuating and counterproductive. Whenever I express my complaints in the hope of evoking pity and receiving the satisfaction I so much desire, the result is always the opposite of what I tried to get. A complainer is hard to live with, and very few people know how to respond to the complaints made by a self-rejecting person. The tragedy is that, often, the complaint, once expressed, leads to that which is most feared: further rejection.

From this perspective, the elder son's inability to share in the joy of his father becomes quite understandable. When he came home from the fields, he heard music and dancing. He knew there was joy in the household. Immediately, he became suspicious. Once the self-rejecting complaint has formed in us, we lose our spontaneity to the extent that even joy can no longer evoke joy in us.

The story says: "Calling one of the servants, he asked what it was all about." There is the fear that I am excluded again, that someone didn't tell me what was going on, that I was kept out of things. The complaint resurges immediately: "Why was I not informed, what is this all about?" The unsuspecting servant, full of excitement and eager to share the good news, explains: "Your brother has come, and your father has killed the calf we had been fattening because he has got him back safe and sound." But this shout of joy cannot be received. Instead of relief and gratitude, the servant's joy summons up the opposite: "He was angry then and refused to go in." Joy and resentment cannot coexist. The music and dancing, instead of inviting to joy, become a cause for even greater withdrawal.

I have very vivid memories of a similar situation. Once, when I felt quite lonely, I asked a friend to go out with me. Although he replied that he didn't have time, I found him just a little later at a mutual friend's house where a party was going on. Seeing me, he said, "Welcome, join us, good to see you." But my anger was so great at not being told about the party that I couldn't stay. All of my inner complaints about not being accepted, liked, and loved surged up in me, and I left the room, slamming the door behind me. I was completely incapacitated—unable to receive and participate in the joy that was there. In an instant, the joy in that room had become a source of resentment.

This experience of not being able to enter into joy is the experience of a resentful heart. The elder son couldn't enter into the house and share in his father's joy. His inner complaint paralyzed him and let the darkness engulf him.

Rembrandt sensed the deepest meaning of this when he painted the elder son at the side of the platform where the younger son is received in the father's joy. He didn't depict the celebration, with its musicians and dancers; they were merely the external signs of the father's joy. The only sign of a party is the relief of a seated flute player carved into the wall against which one of the women (the prodigal's mother?) leans. In place of the party, Rembrandt painted light, the radiant light that envelops both father and son. The joy that Rembrandt portrays is the still joy that belongs to God's house.

In the story one can imagine the elder son standing outside in the dark, not wanting to enter the lighted house filled with happy noises. But Rembrandt paints neither the house nor the fields. He portrays it all with darkness and light. The father's embrace, full of light, is God's house. All the music and dancing are there. The elder son stands outside the circle of this love, refusing to enter. The light on his face makes it clear that he, too, is called to the light, but he cannot be forced.

Sometimes, people wonder: Whatever happened to the elder son? Did he let himself be persuaded by his father? Did he finally enter into the house and participate in the celebration? Did he embrace his brother and welcome him home as his father had done? Did he sit down with the father and his brother at the same table and enjoy with them the festive meal?

Neither Rembrandt's painting nor the parable it portrays tells us about the elder son's final willingness to let himself be found. Is the elder son willing to confess that he, too, is a sinner in need of forgiveness? Is he willing to acknowledge that he is not better than his brother?

I am left alone with these questions. Just as I do not know how the younger son accepted the celebration or how he lived with his father after his return, I also do not know whether the elder son ever reconciled himself with his brother, his father, or himself. What I do know with unwavering certainty is the heart of the father. It is a heart of limitless mercy.

An Open-ended Question

Unlike a fairy tale, the parable provides no happy ending. Instead, it leaves us face to face with one of life's hardest spiritual choices: to trust or not to trust in God's all-forgiving love. I myself am the only one who can make that choice. In response to their complaint, "This man welcomes sinners and eats with them," Jesus confronted the Pharisees and scribes not only with the return of the prodigal son, but also with the resentful elder son. It must have come as a shock to these dutiful religious people. They finally had to face their own complaint and choose how they would respond to God's love for the sinners. Would they be willing to join them at the table as Jesus did? It was and still is a real challenge: for them, for me, for every human being who is caught in resentment and tempted to settle on a complaintive way of life.

The more I reflect on the elder son in me, the more I realize how deeply rooted this form of lostness really is and how hard it is to return home from there. Returning home from a lustful escapade seems so much easier than returning home from a cold anger that has rooted itself in the deepest corners of my being. My resentment is not something that can be easily distinguished and dealt with rationally.

It is far more pernicious: something that has attached itself to the underside of my virtue. Isn't it good to be obedient, dutiful, law-abiding, hardworking, and self-sacrificing? And still it seems that my resentments and complaints are mysteriously tied to such praiseworthy attitudes. This connection often makes me despair. At the very moment I want to speak or act out of my most generous self, I get caught in anger or resentment. And it seems that just as I want to be most selfless, I find myself obsessed about being loved. Just when I do my utmost to accomplish a task well, I find myself questioning why others do not give themselves as I do. Just when I think I am capable of overcoming my temptations, I feel envy toward those who gave in to theirs. It seems that wherever my virtuous self is, there also is the resentful complainer.

Here, I am faced with my own true poverty. I am totally unable to root out my resentments. They are so deeply anchored in the soil of my inner self that pulling them out seems like self-destruction. How to weed out these resentments without uprooting the virtues as well?

Can the elder son in me come home? Can I be found as the younger son was found? How can I return when I am lost in resentment, when I am caught in jealousy, when I am imprisoned in obedience and duty lived out as slavery? It is clear that alone, by myself, I cannot find myself. More daunting than healing myself as the younger son is healing myself as the elder son. Confronted here with the impossibility of self-redemption, I now understand Jesus' words to Nicodemus: "Do not be surprised when I say: 'You must be born from above.' " Indeed, something has to happen that I myself cannot cause to happen. I cannot be reborn from below; that is, with my own strength, with my own mind, with my own psychological insights. There is no doubt in my mind about this because I have tried so hard in the past to heal myself from my complaints and failed . . . and failed . . . and failed, until I came to the edge of complete emotional collapse and even physical exhaustion. I can only be healed from above, from where God reaches down. What is impossible for me is possible for God. "With God, everything is possible."

6
.

THE
ELDER SON'S
RETURN

The elder son . . . was angry then and refused to go in, and his
father came out and began to urge him to come in . . .

The father said, "My son, you are with me always, and all I
have is yours. But it was only right we should celebrate and
rejoice, because your brother here was dead and has come to life; he
was lost and is found."

A Possible Conversion

The father wants not only his younger son back, but his elder son as
well. The elder son, too, needs to be found and led back into the
house of joy. Will he respond to his father's plea or remain stuck in
his bitterness? Rembrandt, too, leaves the elder brother's final decision open to question. Barbara Joan Haeger writes: "Rembrandt
does not reveal whether he sees the light. As he does not clearly
condemn the elder brother, Rembrandt holds out the hope that he

too will perceive he is a sinner . . . the interpretation of the elder brother's reaction is left up to the viewer."

The open-endedness of the story itself and Rembrandt's depiction of it leave me with much spiritual work to do. As I look at the lighted face of the elder son, and then at his darkened hands, I sense not only his captivity, but also the possibility of liberation. This is not a story that separates the two brothers into the good and the evil one. The father only is good. He loves both sons. He runs out to meet both. He wants both to sit at his table and participate in his joy. The younger brother allows himself to be held in a forgiving embrace. The elder brother stands back, looks at the father's merciful gesture, and cannot yet step over his anger and let his father heal him as well.

The Father's love does not force itself on the beloved. Although he wants to heal us of all our inner darkness, we are still free to make our own choice to stay in the darkness or to step into the light of God's love. God is there. God's light is there. God's forgiveness is there. God's boundless love is there. What is so clear is that God is always there, always ready to give and forgive, absolutely independent of our response. God's love does not depend on our repentance or our inner or outer changes.

Whether I am the younger son or the elder son, God's only desire is to bring me home. Arthur Freeman writes:

> The father loves each son and gives each the freedom to be what he can, but he cannot give them freedom they will not take nor adequately understand. The father seems to realize, beyond the customs of his society, the need of his sons to be themselves. But he also knows their need for his love and a "home." How their stories will be completed is up to them. The fact that the parable is not completed makes it certain that the father's love is not dependent upon an appropriate completion of the story. The father's love is only dependent on himself and remains part of his character. As Shakespeare says in one of his sonnets: "Love is not love which alters when it alteration finds."

For me, personally, the possible conversion of the elder son is of crucial importance. There is much in me of that group of which Jesus is most critical: the Pharisees and the scribes. I have studied the books, learned about the laws, and often presented myself as an authority in religious matters. People have shown me a great deal of respect and even called me "reverend." I have been rewarded with compliments and praise, with money and prizes, and with much acclaim. I have been critical of many types of behavior and often passed judgment on others.

So when Jesus tells the parable of the prodigal son, I have to listen with the awareness that I am closest to those who elicited the story from him with the remark: "This man welcomes sinners and eats with them." Is there any chance for me to return to the Father and feel welcome in his home? Or am I so ensnared in my own self-righteous complaints that I am doomed, against my own desire, to remain outside of the house, wallowing in my anger and resentment?

Jesus says: "How blessed are you when you are poor . . . blessed are you who are hungry . . . blessed are you who are weeping . . . ," but I am not poor, hungry, or weeping. Jesus prays: "I bless you Father, Lord of heaven and of earth, for hiding these things [of the kingdom] from the learned and the clever." It is to these, the learned and the clever, that I clearly belong. Jesus shows a distinct preference for those who are marginal in society—the poor, the sick, and the sinners—but I am certainly not marginal. The painful question that arises for me out of the Gospel is: "Have I already had my reward?" Jesus is very critical of those who "say their prayers standing up in their synagogues and at street corners for people to see them." Of them, he says: "In truth I tell you, they have had their reward." With all my writing and speaking about prayer and with all the publicity that I enjoy, I cannot help but wonder if these words are not meant for me.

Indeed they are. But the story of the elder son puts all of these agonizing questions in a new light, making it very plain that God does not love the younger son more than the elder. In the story the father goes out to the elder son just as he did to the younger, urges him to come in, and says, "My son, you are with me always, and all I have is yours."

These are the words I must pay attention to and allow to penetrate to the center of my self. God calls me "my son." The Greek word for son that Luke uses here is *teknon*, "an affectionate form of address," as Joseph A. Fitzmyer says. Literally translated, what the father says is "child."

This affectionate approach becomes even clearer in the words that follow. The harsh and bitter reproaches of the son are not met with words of judgment. There is no recrimination or accusation. The father does not defend himself or even comment on the elder son's behavior. The father moves directly beyond all evaluations to stress his intimate relationship with his son when he says: "You are with me always." The father's declaration of unqualified love eliminates any possibility that the younger son is more loved than the elder. The elder son has never left the house. The father has shared everything with him. He has made him part of his daily life, keeping nothing from him. "All I have is yours," he says. There could be no clearer statement of the father's unlimited love for his elder son. Thus the father's unreserved, unlimited love is offered wholly and equally to both his sons.

Letting Go of Rivalry

The joy at the dramatic return of the younger son in no way means that the elder son was less loved, less appreciated, less favored. The father does not compare the two sons. He loves them both with a complete love and expresses that love according to their individual journeys. He knows them both intimately. He understands their highly unique gifts and shortcomings. He sees with love the passion of his younger son, even when it is not regulated by obedience. With the same love, he sees the obedience of the elder son, even when it is not vitalized by passion. With the younger son there are no thoughts of better or worse, more or less, just as there are no measuring sticks with the elder son. The father responds to both according to their uniqueness. The return of the younger son makes him call for a joyful celebration. The return of the elder son makes him extend an invitation to full participation in that joy.

"In the house of my father there are many places to live," Jesus says. Each child of God has there his or her unique place, all of them places of God. I have to let go of all comparison, all rivalry and competition, and surrender to the Father's love. This requires a leap of faith because I have little experience of non-comparing love and do not know the healing power of such a love. As long as I stay outside in the darkness, I can only remain in the resentful complaint that results from my comparisons. Outside of the light, my younger brother seems to be more loved by the Father than I; in fact, outside of the light, I cannot even see him as my own brother.

God is urging me to come home, to enter into his light, and to discover there that, in God, all people are uniquely and completely loved. In the light of God I can finally see my neighbor as my brother, as the one who belongs as much to God as I do. But outside of God's house, brothers and sisters, husbands and wives, lovers and friends become rivals and even enemies; each perpetually plagued by jealousies, suspicions, and resentments.

It is not surprising that, in his anger, the elder son complains to the father: ". . . you never offered me so much as a kid for me to celebrate with my friends. But, for this son of yours, when he comes back after swallowing up your property—he and his loose women— you kill the calf we had been fattening." These words reveal how deeply hurt this man must feel. His self-esteem is painfully wounded by his father's joy, and his own anger prevents him from accepting this returning scoundrel as his brother. With the words "this son of yours" he distances himself from his brother as well as from his father.

He looks at the two of them as aliens who have lost all sense of reality and engage in a relationship that is completely inappropriate, considering the true facts of the prodigal's life. The elder son no longer has a brother. Nor, any longer, a father. Both have become strangers to him. His brother, a sinner, he looks down on with disdain; his father, a slave owner, he looks up at with fear.

Here I see how lost the elder son is. He has become a foreigner in his own house. True communion is gone. Every relationship is pervaded by the darkness. To be afraid or to show disdain, to suffer submission or to enforce control, to be an oppressor or to be a victim: these have become the choices for one outside of the light. Sins cannot be confessed, forgiveness cannot be received, the mutuality of love cannot exist. True communion has become impossible.

I know the pain of this predicament. In it, everything loses its spontaneity. Everything becomes suspect, self-conscious, calculated, and full of second-guessing. There is no longer any trust. Each little move calls for a countermove; each little remark begs for analysis; the smallest gesture has to be evaluated. This is the pathology of the darkness.

Is there a way out? I don't think there is—at least not on my side. It often seems that the more I try to disentangle myself from the darkness, the darker it becomes. I need light, but that light has to conquer my darkness, and that I cannot bring about myself. I cannot forgive myself. I cannot make myself feel loved. By myself I cannot leave the land of my anger. I cannot bring myself home nor can I create communion on my own. I can desire it, hope for it, wait for it, yes, pray for it. But my true freedom I cannot fabricate for myself. That must be given to me. I am lost. I must be found and brought home by the shepherd who goes out to me.

The story of the prodigal son is the story of a God who goes searching for me and who doesn't rest until he has found me. He urges and he pleads. He begs me to stop clinging to the powers of death and to let myself be embraced by arms that will carry me to the place where I will find the life I most desire.

Recently I lived, very concretely in my own flesh, the return of the elder son. While hitchhiking, I was hit by a car and soon found myself in a hospital close to death. There I suddenly had the illuminating insight that I would not be free to die as long as I was still holding on to the complaint of not having been loved enough by the one whose son I am. I realized that I had not yet grown up completely. I felt strongly the call to lay to rest my adolescent complaints and to give up the lie that I am less loved than my younger brothers. It was frightening, but very liberating. When my dad, far advanced in years, flew over from Holland to visit me, I knew that this was the moment to claim my own God-given sonship. For the first time in my life, I told my father explicitly that I loved him and was grateful for his love for me. I said many things that I had never said before and was surprised at how long it had taken me to say them. My father was somewhat surprised and even puzzled by it all, but received my words with understanding and a smile. As I look back on this spiritual event, I see it as a true return, the return from a false dependence on a human father who cannot give me all I need to a true dependence on the divine Father who says: "You are with me always, and all I have is yours"; the return also from my complaining, comparing, resentful self to my true self that is free to give and receive love. And even though there have been, and undoubtedly will continue to be, many setbacks, it brought me to the beginning of the freedom to live my own life and die my own death. The return to the "Father from whom all fatherhood takes its name" allows me to let my dad be no less than the good, loving, but limited human being he is, and to let my heavenly Father be the God whose unlimited, unconditional love melts away all resentments and anger and makes me free to love beyond the need to please or find approval.

Through Trust and Gratitude

This personal experience of the return of the elder son in me may offer some hope to people caught in the resentment that is the bitter fruit of their need to please. I guess that all of us will someday have to deal with the elder son or the elder daughter in us. The question before us is simply: What can we do to make the return possible? Although God himself runs out to us to find us and bring us home, we must not only recognize that we are lost, but also be prepared to be found and brought home. How? Obviously not by just waiting and being passive. Although we are incapable of liberating ourselves from our frozen anger, we can allow ourselves to be found by God and healed by his love through the concrete and daily practice of trust and gratitude. Trust and gratitude are the disciplines for the conversion of the elder son. And I have come to know them through my own experience.

Without trust, I cannot let myself be found. Trust is that deep inner conviction that the Father wants me home. As long as I doubt that I am worth finding and put myself down as less loved than my younger brothers and sisters, I cannot be found. I have to keep saying to myself, "God is looking for you. He will go anywhere to find you. He loves you, he wants you home, he cannot rest unless he has you with him."

There is a very strong, dark voice in me that says the opposite: "God isn't really interested in me, he prefers the repentant sinner who comes home after his wild escapades. He doesn't pay attention to me who has never left the house. He takes me for granted. I am not his favorite son. I don't expect him to give me what I really want."

At times this dark voice is so strong that I need enormous spiritual energy to trust that the Father wants me home as much as he does the younger son. It requires a real discipline to step over my chronic complaint and to think, speak, and act with the conviction that I am being sought and will be found. Without such discipline, I become prey to self-perpetuating hopelessness.

By telling myself that I am not important enough to be found, I amplify my self-complaint until I have become totally deaf to the voice calling for me. At some point, I must totally disown my self-rejecting voice and claim the truth that God does indeed want to embrace me as much as he does my wayward brothers and sisters. To prevail, this trust has to be even deeper than the sense of lostness. Jesus expresses its radicalness when he says: "Everything you ask and pray for, trust that you have it already, and it will be yours." Living in this radical trust will open the way for God to realize my deepest desire.

Along with trust there must be gratitude—the opposite of resentment. Resentment and gratitude cannot coexist, since resentment blocks the perception and experience of life as a gift. My resentment tells me that I don't receive what I deserve. It always manifests itself in envy.

Gratitude, however, goes beyond the "mine" and "thine" and claims the truth that all of life is a pure gift. In the past I always thought of gratitude as a spontaneous response to the awareness of gifts received, but now I realize that gratitude can also be lived as a discipline. The discipline of gratitude is the explicit effort to acknowledge that all I am and have is given to me as a gift of love, a gift to be celebrated with joy.

Gratitude as a discipline involves a conscious choice. I can choose to be grateful even when my emotions and feelings are still steeped in hurt and resentment. It is amazing how many occasions present themselves in which I can choose gratitude instead of a complaint. I can choose to be grateful when I am criticized, even when my heart still responds in bitterness. I can choose to speak about goodness and beauty, even when my inner eye still looks for someone to accuse or something to call ugly. I can choose to listen to the voices that forgive and to look at the faces that smile, even while I still hear words of revenge and see grimaces of hatred.

There is always the choice between resentment and gratitude because God has appeared in my darkness, urged me to come home, and declared in a voice filled with affection: "You are with me always, and all I have is yours." Indeed, I can choose to dwell in the darkness in which I stand, point to those who are seemingly better off than I, lament about the many misfortunes that have plagued me in the past, and thereby wrap myself up in my resentment. But I don't have to do this. There is the option to look into the eyes of the One who came out to search for me and see therein that all I am and all I have is pure gift calling for gratitude.

The choice for gratitude rarely comes without some real effort.

But each time I make it, the next choice is a little easier, a little freer, a little less self-conscious. Because every gift I acknowledge reveals another and another until, finally, even the most normal, obvious, and seemingly mundane event or encounter proves to be filled with grace. There is an Estonian proverb that says: "Who does not thank for little will not thank for much." Acts of gratitude make one grateful because, step by step, they reveal that all is grace.

Both trust and gratitude require the courage to take risks because distrust and resentment, in their need to keep their claim on me, keep warning me how dangerous it is to let go of my careful calculations and guarded predictions. At many points I have to make a leap of faith to let trust and gratitude have a chance: to write a gentle letter to someone who will not forgive me, make a call to someone who has rejected me, speak a word of healing to someone who cannot do the same.

The leap of faith always means loving without expecting to be loved in return, giving without wanting to receive, inviting without hoping to be invited, holding without asking to be held. And every time I make a little leap, I catch a glimpse of the One who runs out to me and invites me into his joy, the joy in which I can find not only myself, but also my brothers and sisters. Thus the disciplines of trust and gratitude reveal the God who searches for me, burning with desire to take away all my resentments and complaints and to let me sit at his side at the heavenly banquet.

The True Elder Son

The return of the elder son is becoming as important to me *as*—if not more important *than*—the return of the younger son. How will the elder son look when he is free from his complaints, free from his anger, resentments, and jealousies? Because the parable tells us nothing about the response of the elder son, we are left with the choice of listening to the Father or of remaining imprisoned in our self-rejection.

But even as I reflect on that choice and realize that the whole parable was told by Jesus and painted by Rembrandt for my conversion, it becomes clear to me that Jesus, who told the story, is himself not only the younger son, but the elder son as well. He has come to show the Father's love and to free me from the bondage of my resentments. All that Jesus says about himself reveals him as the Beloved Son, the one who lives in complete communion with the Father. There is no distance, fear, or suspicion between Jesus and the Father.

The words of the father in the parable: "My son, you are with me always, and all I have is yours" express the true relationship of God the Father with Jesus his Son. Jesus constantly affirms that all the glory that belongs to the Father belongs to the Son too. All the Father does, the Son does too. There is no separation between Father and Son: "The Father and I are one"; no division of work: "The Father loves the Son and has entrusted everything to him"; no competition: "I have made known to you everything I have learned from my Father"; no envy: "The Son can do nothing by himself, he can do only what he sees the Father doing." There is perfect unity between Father and Son. This unity belongs at the center of Jesus' message: "You must believe me when I say that I am in the Father and the Father is in me." To believe in Jesus means to believe that he is the one sent by the Father, the one in and through whom the fullness of the Father's love is revealed.

This is expressed dramatically by Jesus himself in the parable of the wicked tenants. The owner of the vineyard, after having sent in vain several stewards to collect his share of the harvest, decides to send "his beloved son." The tenants recognize that he is the heir and kill him to obtain the inheritance for themselves. This is the picture of the true son who obeys his father, not as a slave, but as the Beloved, and fulfills the will of the Father in full unity with him.

Thus Jesus is the elder Son of the Father. He is sent by the Father to reveal God's unremitting love for all his resentful children and to offer himself as the way home. Jesus is God's way of making the impossible possible—of allowing light to conquer darkness. Resentments and complaints, deep as they may seem, can vanish in the face of him in whom the full light of Sonship is visible. As I look again at Rembrandt's elder son, I realize that the cold light on his face can become deep and warm—transforming him totally—and make him who he truly is: "The Beloved Son on whom God's favor rests."

While he was still a long way off, his father saw him and was moved with pity. He ran to the boy, clasped him in his arms and kissed him . . . the father said to his servants, "Quick! Bring out the best robe and put it on him; put a ring on his finger and sandals on his feet. Bring the calf we have been fattening, and kill it; we will celebrate by having a feast, because this son of mine was dead and has come back to life; he was lost and is found." And they began to celebrate.

. . . his father came out and began to urge him to come in . . . The father said, "My son, you are with me always, and all I have is yours. But it was only right we should celebrate and rejoice, because your brother here was dead and has come to life; he was lost and is found."

7.

REMBRANDT
AND THE FATHER

While I was sitting in front of the painting in the Hermitage trying to absorb what I saw, many groups of tourists passed by. Even though they spent less than a minute with the painting, almost all of the guides described it as a painting of the compassionate father, and most of them mentioned that it was one of Rembrandt's last paintings, one to which he came only after a life of suffering. Indeed, this is what this painting is all about. It is the human expression of divine compassion.

Instead of its being called *The Return of the Prodigal Son,* it could easily have been called "The Welcome by the Compassionate Father." The emphasis is less on the son than on the father. The parable is in truth a "Parable of the Father's Love." Looking at the way in which Rembrandt portrays the father, there came to me a whole new interior understanding of tenderness, mercy, and forgiveness. Seldom, if ever, has God's immense, compassionate love been expressed in such a poignant way. Every detail of the father's figure—his facial expression, his posture, the colors of his dress, and, most of all, the still gesture of his hands—speaks of the divine love for humanity that existed from the beginning and ever will be.

Everything comes together here: Rembrandt's story, humanity's story, and God's story. Time and eternity intersect; approaching death and everlasting life touch each other. Sin and forgiveness embrace; the human and the divine become one.

What gives Rembrandt's portrayal of the father such an irresistible power is that the most divine is captured in the most human. I see a half-blind old man with a mustache and a parted beard, dressed in a gold-embroidered garment and a deep red cloak, laying his large, stiffened hands on the shoulders of his returning son. This is very specific, concrete, and describable.

I also see, however, infinite compassion, unconditional love, everlasting forgiveness—divine realities—emanating from a Father who is the creator of the universe. Here, both the human and the divine, the fragile and the powerful, the old and the eternally young are fully expressed. This is Rembrandt's genius. The spiritual truth is completely enfleshed. As Paul Baudiquet writes: "The spiritual in Rembrandt . . . pulls its strongest and most splendid accents from the flesh."

It is of special significance that Rembrandt chose a nearly blind old man to communicate God's love. Surely the parable Jesus told and the way the parable has been interpreted throughout the centuries offer the main basis for the portrayal of God's merciful love. But I should not forget that it was Rembrandt's own story that enabled him to give it its unique expression.

Paul Baudiquet says: "Since his youth, Rembrandt has had but one vocation: to grow old." And it is true that Rembrandt always displayed a great interest in older people. He had drawn them, etched them, and painted them ever since he was a young man and became increasingly fascinated by their inner beauty. Some of Rembrandt's most stunning portraits are of old people, and his most gripping self-portraits are made during his last years.

After his many trials at home and at work, he shows a special fascination with blind people. As the light in his work interiorizes, he begins to paint blind people as the real see-ers. He is attracted to Tobit and the near-blind Simeon, and he paints them several times.

As Rembrandt's own life moves toward the shadows of old age, as his success wanes, and the exterior splendor of his life diminishes, he comes more in touch with the immense beauty of the interior life. There he discovers the light that comes from an inner fire that never dies: the fire of love. His art no longer tries to "grasp, conquer, and regulate the visible," but to "transform the visible in the fire of love that comes from the unique heart of the artist."

The unique heart of Rembrandt becomes the unique heart of the father. The inner, light-giving fire of love that has grown strong through the artist's many years of suffering burns in the heart of the father who welcomes his returning son.

I understand now why Rembrandt didn't follow the literal text of the parable. There St. Luke writes: "While the younger son was still a long way off, his father saw him and was moved with pity. He ran to the boy, clasped him in his arms and kissed him." Earlier in his life, Rembrandt had etched and drawn this event with all the dramatic movement it contains. But as he approached death, Rembrandt chose to portray a very still father who recognizes his son, not with the eyes of the body, but with the inner eye of his heart.

It seems that the hands that touch the back of the returning son are the instruments of the father's inner eye. The near-blind father sees far and wide. His seeing is an eternal seeing, a seeing that reaches out to all of humanity. It is a seeing that understands the lostness of women and men of all times and places, that knows with immense compassion the suffering of those who have chosen to leave home, that cried oceans of tears as they got caught in anguish and agony.

The heart of the father burns with an immense desire to bring his children home.

Oh, how much would he have liked to talk to them, to warn them against the many dangers they were facing, and to convince them that at home can be found everything that they search for elsewhere. How much would he have liked to pull them back with his fatherly authority and hold them close to himself so that they would not get hurt.

But his love is too great to do any of that. It cannot force, constrain, push, or pull. It offers the freedom to reject that love or to love in return. It is precisely the immensity of the divine love that is the source of the divine suffering. God, creator of heaven and earth, has chosen to be, first and foremost, a Father.

As Father, he wants his children to be free, free to love. That freedom includes the possibility of their leaving home, going to a "distant country," and losing everything. The Father's heart knows all the pain that will come from that choice, but his love makes him powerless to prevent it. As Father, he desires that those who stay at home enjoy his presence and experience his affection. But here again, he wants only to offer a love that can be freely received. He suffers beyond telling when his children honor him only with lip service, while their hearts are far from him. He knows their "deceitful tongues" and "disloyal hearts," but he cannot make them love him without losing his true fatherhood.

As Father, the only authority he claims for himself is the authority of compassion. That authority comes from letting the sins of his children pierce his heart. There is no lust, greed, anger, resentment, jealousy, or vengeance in his lost children that has not caused immense grief to his heart. The grief is so deep because the heart is so pure. From the deep inner place where love embraces all human grief, the Father reaches out to his children. The touch of his hands, radiating inner light, seeks only to heal.

Here is the God I want to believe in: a Father who, from the beginning of creation, has stretched out his arms in merciful blessing, never forcing himself on anyone, but always waiting; never letting his arms drop down in despair, but always hoping that his children will return so that he can speak words of love to them and let his tired arms rest on their shoulders. His only desire is to bless.

In Latin, to bless is *benedicere,* which means literally: saying good things. The Father wants to say, more with his touch than with his voice, good things of his children. He has no desire to punish them. They have already been punished excessively by their own inner or outer waywardness. The Father wants simply to let them know that the love they have searched for in such distorted ways has been, is, and always will be there for them. The Father wants to say, more with his hands than with his mouth: "You are my Beloved, on you my favor rests." He is the shepherd, "feeding his flock, gathering lambs in his arms, holding them against his breast."

The true center of Rembrandt's painting is the hands of the father. On them all the light is concentrated; on them the eyes of the bystanders are focused; in them mercy becomes flesh; upon them forgiveness, reconciliation, and healing come together, and, through them, not only the tired son, but also the worn-out father find their rest. From the moment I first saw the poster on Simone's office door, I felt drawn to those hands. I did not fully understand why. But gradually over the years I have come to know those hands. They have held me from the hour of my conception, they welcomed me at my birth, held me close to my mother's breast, fed me, and kept me warm. They have protected me in times of danger and consoled me in times of grief. They have waved me good-bye and always welcomed me back. Those hands are God's hands. They are also the hands of my parents, teachers, friends, healers, and all those whom God has given me to remind me how safely I am held.

Not long after Rembrandt painted the father and his blessing hands, he died.

Rembrandt's hands had painted countless human faces and human hands. In this, one of his last paintings, he painted the face and the hands of God. Who had posed for this life-size portrait of God? Rembrandt himself?

The father of the prodigal son *is* a self-portrait, but not in the traditional sense. Rembrandt's own face appears in several of his paintings. It appears as the prodigal son in the brothel, as a frightened disciple on the lake, as one of the men taking the dead body of Jesus from the cross.

Yet here it is not Rembrandt's face that is reflected, but his soul, the soul of a father who had suffered so many a death. During his sixty-three years, Rembrandt saw not only his dear wife Saskia die, but also three sons, two daughters, and the two women with whom he lived. The grief for his beloved son Titus, who died at the age of twenty-six shortly after his marriage, has never been described, but in the father of the *Prodigal Son* we can see how many tears it must have cost him. Created in the image of God, Rembrandt had come to discover through his long, painful struggle the true nature of that image. It is the image of a near-blind old man crying tenderly, blessing his deeply wounded son. Rembrandt was the son, he became the father, and thus was made ready to enter eternal life.

8

·

THE
FATHER WELCOMES
HOME

While he was still a long way off, his father saw him [his younger son] and was moved with pity. He ran to the boy, clasped him in his arms and kissed him.

. . . his father came out and began to urge him [his elder son] to come in.

Father and Mother

Often I have asked friends to give me their first impression of Rembrandt's *Prodigal Son*. Inevitably, they point to the wise old man who forgives his son: the benevolent patriarch.

The longer I looked at "the patriarch," the clearer it became to me that Rembrandt had done something quite different from letting God pose as the wise old head of a family. It all began with the hands. The two are quite different. The father's left hand touching the son's shoulder is strong and muscular. The fingers are spread out and cover a large part of the prodigal son's shoulder and back. I can see a certain pressure, especially in the thumb. That hand seems not only to touch, but, with its strength, also to hold. Even though there is a gentleness in the way the father's left hand touches his son, it is not without a firm grip.

How different is the father's right hand! This hand does not hold or grasp. It is refined, soft, and very tender. The fingers are close to each other and they have an elegant quality. It lies gently upon the son's shoulder. It wants to caress, to stroke, and to offer consolation and comfort. It is a mother's hand.

Some commentators have suggested that the masculine left hand is Rembrandt's own hand, while the feminine right hand is similar to the right hand of *The Jewish Bride* painted in the same period. I like to believe that this is true.

As soon as I recognized the difference between the two hands of the father, a new world of meaning opened up for me. The Father is not simply a great patriarch. He is mother as well as father. He touches the son with a masculine hand and a feminine hand. He holds, and she caresses. He confirms and she consoles. He is, indeed, God, in whom both manhood and womanhood, fatherhood and motherhood, are fully present. That gentle caressing right hand echoes for me the words of the prophet Isaiah: "Can a woman forget her baby at the breast, feel no pity for the child she has borne? Even if these were to forget, I shall not forget you. Look, I have engraved you on the palms of my hands."

My friend Richard White pointed out to me that the caressing feminine hand of the father parallels the bare, wounded foot of the son, while the strong masculine hand parallels the foot dressed in a sandal. Is it too much to think that the one hand protects the vulnerable side of the son, while the other hand reinforces the son's strength and desire to get on with his life?

Then there is the great red cloak. With its warm color and its arch-like shape, it offers a welcome place where it is good to be. At first, the cloak covering the bent-over body of the father looked to me like a tent inviting the tired traveler to find some rest. But as I went on gazing at the red cloak, another image, stronger than that of a tent, came to me: the sheltering wings of the mother bird. They reminded me of Jesus' words about God's maternal love: "Jerusalem, Jerusalem . . . How often have I longed to gather your children, as a hen gathers her chicks under her wings, and you refused!"

Day and night God holds me safe, as a hen holds her chicks secure under her wings. Even more than that of a tent, the image of a vigilant mother bird's wings expresses the safety that God offers her children. They express care, protection, a place to rest and feel safe.

Every time I look at the tent-like and wings-like cloak in Rembrandt's painting, I sense the motherly quality of God's love and my heart begins to sing in words inspired by the Psalmist:

> You who dwell in the shelter of the Most High
> and abide in the shade of the Almighty—
> say to your God: "My refuge, my stronghold,
> my God in whom I trust!
> . . . You conceal me with your pinions
> and under your wings I shall find refuge."

And so, under the aspect of an old Jewish patriarch, there emerges also a motherly God receiving her son home.

As I now look again at Rembrandt's old man bending over his returning son and touching his shoulders with his hands, I begin to see not only a father who "clasps his son in his arms," but also a mother who caresses her child, surrounds him with the warmth of her body, and holds him against the womb from which he sprang. Thus the "return of the prodigal son" becomes the return to God's womb, the return to the very origins of being and again echoes Jesus' exhortation to Nicodemus, to be reborn from above.

Now I understand better also the enormous stillness of this portrait of God. There is no sentimentality here, no romanticism, no simplistic tale with a happy ending. What I see here is God as mother, receiving back into her womb the one whom she made in her own image. The near-blind eyes, the hands, the cloak, the bent-

over body, they all call forth the divine maternal love, marked by grief, desire, hope, and endless waiting.

The mystery, indeed, is that God in her infinite compassion has linked herself for eternity with the life of her children. She has freely chosen to become dependent on her creatures, whom she has gifted with freedom. This choice causes her grief when they leave; this choice brings her gladness when they return. But her joy will not be complete until all who have received life from her have returned home and gather together around the table prepared for them.

And this includes the elder son. Rembrandt places him at a distance, out from under the billowing cloak, at the edge of the circle of light. The elder son's dilemma is to accept or reject that his father's love is beyond comparisons; to dare to be loved as his father longs to love him or to insist on being loved as *he* feels he ought to be loved. The father knows that the choice must be the son's, even while he waits with outstretched hands. Will the elder son be willing to kneel and be touched by the same hands that touch his younger brother? Will he be willing to be forgiven and to experience the healing presence of the father who loves him beyond compare? Luke's story makes it very clear that the father goes out to both of his children. Not only does he run out to welcome the younger wayward son, but he comes out also to meet the elder, dutiful son as he returns from the fields wondering what the music and dancing are all about and urges him to come in.

No More or Less

It is very important for me to understand the full meaning of what is happening here. While the father is truly filled with joy at his younger son's return, he has not forgotten the elder. He doesn't take his elder son for granted. His joy was so intense that he couldn't wait to start celebrating, but as soon as he became aware of his elder son's arrival, he left the party, went out to him, and pleaded with him to join them.

In his jealousy and bitterness, the elder son can only see that his irresponsible brother is receiving more attention than he himself, and concludes that he is the less loved of the two. His father's heart, however, is not divided into more or less. The father's free and spontaneous response to his younger son's return does not involve any comparisons with his elder son. To the contrary, he ardently desires to make his elder son part of his joy.

This is not easy for me to grasp. In a world that constantly compares people, ranking them as more or less intelligent, more or less attractive, more or less successful, it is not easy to really believe in a love that does not do the same. When I hear someone praised, it is hard not to think of myself as less praiseworthy; when I read about the goodness and kindness of other people, it is hard not to wonder whether I myself am as good and kind as they; and when I see trophies, rewards, and prizes being handed out to special people, I cannot avoid asking myself why that didn't happen to me.

The world in which I have grown up is a world so full of grades, scores, and statistics that, consciously or unconsciously, I always try to take my measure against all the others. Much sadness and gladness in my life flows directly from my comparing, and most, if not all, of this comparing is useless and a terrible waste of time and energy.

Our God, who is both Father and Mother to us, does not compare. Never. Even though I know in my head that this is true, it is still very hard to fully accept it with my whole being. When I hear someone called a favorite son or daughter, my immediate response is that the other children must be less appreciated, or less loved. I cannot fathom how all of God's children can be favorites. And still, they are. When I look from my place in the world into God's Kingdom, I quickly come to think of God as the keeper of some great celestial scoreboard, and I will always be afraid of not making the grade. But as soon as I look from God's welcoming home into the world, I discover that God loves with a divine love, a love that cedes to all women and men their uniqueness without ever comparing.

The elder brother compares himself with the younger one and becomes jealous. But the father loves them both so much that it didn't even occur to him to delay the party in order to prevent the elder son from feeling rejected. I am convinced that many of my emotional problems would melt as snow in the sun if I could let the truth of God's motherly non-comparing love permeate my heart.

How hard that is becomes clear when I reflect on the parable of the laborers in the vineyard. Each time I read that parable in which the landowner gives as much to the workers who worked only one hour as to those who did "a heavy day's work in all the heat," a feeling of irritation still wells up inside of me.

Why didn't the landowner pay those who worked many long hours first and then surprise the latecomers with his generosity? Why, instead, does he pay the workers of the eleventh hour first, raising false expectations in the others and creating unnecessary bitterness and jealousy? These questions, I now realize, come from a perspective that is all too willing to impose the economy of the temporal on the unique order of the divine.

It hadn't previously occurred to me that the landowner might have wanted the workers of the early hours to rejoice in his generosity to the latecomers. It never crossed my mind that he might have acted on the supposition that those who had worked in the vineyard the whole day would be deeply grateful to have had the opportunity to do work for their boss, and even more grateful to see what a generous man he is. It requires an interior about-face to accept such a non-comparing way of thinking. But that is God's way of thinking. God looks at his people as children of a family who are happy that those who have done only a little bit are as much loved as those who accomplish much.

God is so naive as to think that there would be great rejoicing when all those who spent time in his vineyard, whether a short time or a long time, were given the same attention. Indeed, he was so naive as to expect that they would all be so happy to be in his presence that comparing themselves with each other wouldn't even occur to them. That is why he says with the bewilderment of a misunderstood lover: "Why should you be envious because I am generous?" He could have said: "You have been with me the whole day, and I gave you all you asked for! Why are you so bitter?" It is the same bewilderment that comes from the heart of the father when he says to his jealous son: "My son, you are with me always, and all I have is yours."

Here lies hidden the great call to conversion: to look not with the eyes of my own low self-esteem, but with the eyes of God's love. As long as I keep looking at God as a landowner, as a father who wants to get the most out of me for the least cost, I cannot but become jealous, bitter, and resentful toward my fellow workers or my brothers and sisters. But if I am able to look at the world with the eyes of God's love and discover that God's vision is not that of a stereotypical landowner or patriarch but rather that of an all-giving and forgiving father who does not measure out his love to his children according to how well they behave, then I quickly see that my only true response can be deep gratitude.

The Heart of God

In Rembrandt's painting, the elder son simply observes. It is difficult to imagine what is going on in his heart. Just as with the parable, so also with the painting, I am left with the question: How will he respond to the invitation to join the celebration?

There is no doubt—in the parable or the painting—about the father's heart. His heart goes out to both of his sons; he loves them both; he hopes to see them together as brothers around the same table; he wants them to experience that, different as they are, they belong to the same household and are children of the same father.

As I let all of this sink in, I see how the story of the father and his lost sons powerfully affirms that it was not I who chose God, but God who first chose me. This is the great mystery of our faith. We do not choose God, God chooses us. From all eternity we are hidden "in the shadow of God's hand" and "engraved on his palm." Before any human being touches us, God "forms us in secret" and "textures us" in the depth of the earth, and before any human being decides about us, God "knits us together in our mother's womb." God loves us before any human person can show love to us. He loves us with a "first" love, an unlimited, unconditional love, wants us to be his beloved children, and tells us to become as loving as himself.

For most of my life I have struggled to find God, to know God, to love God. I have tried hard to follow the guidelines of the spiritual life—pray always, work for others, read the Scriptures—and to avoid the many temptations to dissipate myself. I have failed many times but always tried again, even when I was close to despair.

Now I wonder whether I have sufficiently realized that during all this time God has been trying to find me, to know me, and to love me. The question is not "How am I to find God?" but "How am I to let myself be found by him?" The question is not "How am I to know God?" but "How am I to let myself be known by God?" And, finally, the question is not "How am I to love God?" but "How am I to let myself be loved by God?" God is looking into the distance for me, trying to find me, and longing to bring me home. In all three parables which Jesus tells in response to the question of why he eats with sinners, he puts the emphasis on God's initiative. God is the shepherd who goes looking for his lost sheep. God is the woman who lights a lamp, sweeps out the house, and searches everywhere for her lost coin until she has found it. God is the father who watches and waits for his children, runs out to meet them, embraces them, pleads with them, begs and urges them to come home.

It might sound strange, but God wants to find me as much as, if not more than, I want to find God. Yes, God needs me as much as I need God. God is not the patriarch who stays home, doesn't move, and expects his children to come to him, apologize for their aberrant behavior, beg for forgiveness, and promise to do better. To the contrary, he leaves the house, ignoring his dignity by running toward them, pays no heed to apologies and promises of change, and brings them to the table richly prepared for them.

I am beginning now to see how radically the character of my spiritual journey will change when I no longer think of God as hiding out and making it as difficult as possible for me to find him, but, instead, as the one who is looking for me while I am doing the hiding. When I look through God's eyes at my lost self and discover God's joy at my coming home, then my life may become less anguished and more trusting.

Wouldn't it be good to increase God's joy by letting God find me and carry me home and celebrate my return with the angels? Wouldn't it be wonderful to make God smile by giving God the chance to find me and love me lavishly? Questions like these raise a real issue: that of my own self-concept. Can I accept that I am worth looking for? Do I believe that there is a real desire in God to simply be with me?

Here lies the core of my spiritual struggle: the struggle against self-rejection, self-contempt, and self-loathing. It is a very fierce battle because the world and its demons conspire to make me think about myself as worthless, useless, and negligible. Many consumerist economies stay afloat by manipulating the low self-esteem of their consumers and by creating spiritual expectations through material means. As long as I am kept "small," I can easily be seduced to buy things, meet people, or go places that promise a radical change in self-concept even though they are totally incapable of bringing this about. But every time I allow myself to be thus manipulated or seduced, I will have still more reasons for putting myself down and seeing myself as the unwanted child.

A First and Everlasting Love

For a very long time I considered low self-esteem to be some kind of virtue. I had been warned so often against pride and conceit that I came to consider it a good thing to deprecate myself. But now I realize that the real sin is to deny God's first love for me, to ignore my original goodness. Because without claiming that first love and that original goodness for myself, I lose touch with my true self and embark on the destructive search among the wrong people and in the wrong places for what can only be found in the house of my Father.

I do not think I am alone in this struggle to claim God's first love and my original goodness. Beneath much human assertiveness, competitiveness, and rivalry; beneath much self-confidence and even arrogance, there is often a very insecure heart, much less sure of itself than outward behavior would lead one to believe. I have often been shocked to discover that men and women with obvious talents and with many rewards for their accomplishments have so many doubts about their own goodness. Instead of experiencing their outward successes as a sign of their inner beauty, they live them as a cover-up for their sense of personal worthlessness. Not a few have said to me: "If people only knew what goes on in my innermost self, they would stop with their applause and praise."

I vividly remember talking with a young man loved and admired by everyone who knew him. He told me how a small critical remark from one of his friends had thrown him into an abyss of depression. As he spoke, tears streamed from his eyes and his body twisted in anguish. He felt that his friend had broken through his wall of defenses and had seen him as he really was: an ugly hypocrite, a despicable man beneath his gleaming armor. As I heard his story, I realized what an unhappy life he had lived, even though the people around him had envied him for his gifts. For years he had walked around with the inner questions: "Does anyone really love me? Does anyone really care?" And every time he had climbed a little higher on the ladder of success, he had thought: "This is not who I really am; one day everything will come crashing down and then people will see that I am no good."

This encounter illustrates the way many people live their lives— never fully sure that they are loved as they are. Many have horrendous stories that offer very plausible reasons for their low self-esteem: stories about parents who were not giving them what they needed, about teachers who mistreated them, about friends who betrayed them, and about a Church which left them out in the cold during a critical moment of their life.

The parable of the prodigal son is a story that speaks about a love that existed before any rejection was possible and that will still be there after all rejections have taken place. It is the first and everlasting love of a God who is Father as well as Mother. It is the fountain of all true human love, even the most limited. Jesus' whole life and preaching had only one aim: to reveal this inexhaustible, unlimited motherly and fatherly love of his God and to show the way to let that love guide every part of our daily lives. In his painting of the father, Rembrandt offers me a glimpse of that love. It is the love that always welcomes home and always wants to celebrate.

9

.

THE FATHER
CALLS FOR A
CELEBRATION

The father said to his servants, "Quick! Bring out the best robe
and put it on him; put a ring on his finger and sandals on his feet.
Bring the calf we have been fattening, and kill it; we will celebrate
by having a feast, because this son of mine was dead and has come
back to life; he was lost and is found." And they began to
celebrate.

Giving the Very Best

It is clear to me that the younger son is not returning to a simple
farm family. Luke describes the father as a very wealthy man with
extensive property and many servants. To match this description
Rembrandt clothes him and the two men who are watching him
richly. The two women in the background lean against an arch that
looks more like a part of a palace than of a farmhouse. The splendid
garb of the father and the prosperous look of his surroundings stand

in sharp contrast to the long suffering so visible in his near-blind eyes, his sorrowful face, and his stooped figure.

The same God who suffers because of his immense love for his children is the God who is rich in goodness and mercy and who desires to reveal to his children the richness of his glory. The father does not even give his son a chance to apologize. He pre-empts his son's begging by spontaneous forgiveness and puts aside his pleas as completely irrelevant in the light of the joy at his return. But there is more. Not only does the father forgive without asking questions and joyfully welcome his lost son home, but he cannot wait to give him new life, life in abundance. So strongly does God desire to give life to his returning son that he seems almost impatient. Nothing is good enough. The very best must be given to him. While the son is prepared to be treated as a hired servant, the father calls for the robe reserved for a distinguished guest; and, although the son no longer feels worthy to be called son, the father gives him a ring for his finger and sandals for his feet to honor him as his beloved son and restore him as his heir.

I remember vividly the clothes I wore during the summer after my graduation from high school. My white trousers, broad belt, colorful shirt, and shining shoes all expressed how good I felt about myself. My parents were very glad to buy these new clothes for me and showed great pride in their son. And I felt grateful to be their son. I especially recall how good it felt to wear new shoes. Since those days, I have traveled a lot and seen how people go through life barefoot. Now I understand even better the symbolic significance of new shoes. Bare feet indicate poverty and often slavery. Shoes are for the wealthy and the powerful. Shoes offer protection against snakes; they give safety and strength. They turn the hunted ones into hunters. For many poor people, getting shoes is a benchmark passage. An old Afro-American spiritual expresses this beautifully: "All of God's chillun got shoes. When I get to heab'n I'm going to put on my shoes; I'm going to walk all ovah God's heab'n."

The Father dresses his son with the signs of freedom, the freedom of the children of God. He does not want any of them to be hired servants or slaves. He wants them to wear the robe of honor, the ring of inheritance, and the footwear of prestige. It is like an investiture by which God's year of favor is inaugurated. The full meaning of this investiture and inauguration is spelled out in the fourth vision of the prophet Zechariah:

> Yahweh showed me the high priest Joshua standing before the angel of Yahweh. . . . Now Joshua was dressed in dirty clothes as he stood before the angel. The latter then spoke as follows to those who were standing before him. "Take off his dirty clothes and dress him in splendid robes and put a turban on his head." So they put a turban on his head and dressed him in clean clothes, while the angel of Yahweh stood by and said, "You see, I have taken your guilt away." The angel of Yahweh then made this declaration to Joshua: "Yahweh Sabaoth says this, 'If you walk in my ways and keep my ordinances, you shall govern my house, you shall watch over my courts, and I will give you free access among those in attendance here. . . . So listen, High Priest Joshua. . . . I shall remove this country's guilt in a single day. On that day . . . invite each other to come under your vine and your fig tree.' "

As I read the story of the prodigal son with this vision of Zechariah in mind, the word "Quick," with which the father exhorts his servants to bring his son the robe, ring, and sandals, expresses much more than a human impatience. It reveals the divine eagerness to inaugurate the new Kingdom that has been prepared from the beginning of time.

There is no doubt that the father wants a lavish feast. Killing the calf that had been fattened up for a special occasion shows how much the father wanted to pull out all the stops and offer his son a party such as had never been celebrated before. His exuberant joy is obvious. After having given his order to make everything ready, he exclaims: "We will celebrate by having a feast, because this son of mine was dead and has come back to life; he was lost and is found," and immediately they begin to celebrate. There is an abundance of food, there is music and dance, and the happy party noises can be heard far beyond the house.

An Invitation to Joy

I realize that I am not used to the image of God throwing a big party. It seems to contradict the solemnity and seriousness I have always attached to God. But when I think about the ways in which Jesus describes God's Kingdom, a joyful banquet is often at its center. Jesus says, "Many will come from east and west and sit down with Abraham and Isaac and Jacob at the feast in the Kingdom of Heaven." And he compares the Kingdom of Heaven with a wedding feast offered by the king to his son. The king's servants go out to invite people with the words: "Look, my banquet is all prepared, my oxen and fattened cattle have been slaughtered, everything is ready. Come to the wedding." But many were not interested. They were too busy with their own affairs.

Just as in the parable of the prodigal son, Jesus expresses here the great desire of his Father to offer his children a banquet and his eagerness to get it going even when those who are invited refuse to come. This invitation to a meal is an invitation to intimacy with God. This is especially clear at the Last Supper, shortly before Jesus' death. There he says to his disciples: "From now on, I tell you, I shall never again drink wine until the day I drink the new wine with you in the kingdom of my Father." And at the close of the New Testament, God's ultimate victory is described as a splendid wedding feast: "The reign of the Lord our God Almighty has begun; let us be glad and joyful and give glory to God, because this is the time for the marriage of the Lamb. . . . blessed are those who are invited to the wedding feast of the Lamb . . ."

Celebration belongs to God's Kingdom. God not only offers forgiveness, reconciliation, and healing, but wants to lift up these gifts as a source of joy for all who witness them. In all three of the parables which Jesus tells to explain why he eats with sinners, God rejoices and invites others to rejoice with him. "Rejoice with me," the shepherd says, "I have found my sheep that was lost." "Rejoice with me," the woman says, "I have found the drachma I lost." "Rejoice with me," the father says, "this son of mine was lost and is found."

All these voices are the voices of God. God does not want to keep his joy to himself. He wants everyone to share in it. God's joy is the joy of his angels and his saints; it is the joy of all who belong to the Kingdom.

Rembrandt paints the moment of the return of the younger son. The elder son and the three other members of the father's household keep their distance. Will they understand the father's joy? Will they let the father embrace them? Will I? Will they be able to step out of their recriminations and share in the celebration? Will I?

I can see only one moment, and I am left guessing as to what will happen next. I repeat: Will they? Will I? I know the father wants all the people around him to admire the returning son's new clothes, to join him around the table, to eat and dance with him. This is not a private affair. This is something for all in the family to celebrate in gratitude.

I repeat again: Will they? Will I? It is an important question because it touches—strange as it may sound—my resistance to living a joyful life.

God rejoices. Not because the problems of the world have been solved, not because all human pain and suffering have come to an end, nor because thousands of people have been converted and are now praising him for his goodness. No, God rejoices because *one* of his children who was lost has been found. What I am called to is to enter into that joy. It is God's joy, not the joy that the world offers. It is the joy that comes from seeing a child walk home amid all the destruction, devastation, and anguish of the world. It is a hidden joy, as inconspicuous as the flute player that Rembrandt painted in the wall above the head of the seated observer.

I am not accustomed to rejoicing in things that are small, hidden, and scarcely noticed by the people around me. I am generally ready and prepared to receive bad news, to read about wars, violence, and crimes, and to witness conflict and disarray. I always expect my visitors to talk about their problems and pain, their setbacks and disappointments, their depressions and their anguish. Somehow I have become accustomed to living with sadness, and so have lost the eyes to see the joy and the ears to hear the gladness that belongs to God and which is to be found in the hidden corners of the world.

I have a friend who is so deeply connected with God that he can see joy where I expect only sadness. He travels much and meets countless people. When he returns home, I always expect him to tell me about the difficult economic situation of the countries he visited, about the great injustices he heard about, and the pain he has seen. But even though he is very aware of the great upheaval of the world, he seldom speaks of it. When he shares his experiences, he tells about the hidden joys he has discovered. He tells about a man, a woman, or a child who brought him hope and peace. He tells about little groups of people who are faithful to each other in the midst of all the turmoil. He tells about the small wonders of God. At times I realize that I am disappointed because I want to hear "newspaper news," exciting and exhilarating stories that can be talked about among friends. But he never responds to my need for sensationalism. He keeps saying: "I saw something very small and very beautiful, something that gave me much joy."

The father of the prodigal son gives himself totally to the joy that his returning son brings him. I have to learn from that. I have to learn to "steal" all the real joy there is to steal and lift it up for others to see. Yes, I know that not everybody has been converted yet, that there is not yet peace everywhere, that all pain has not yet been taken away, but still, I see people turning and returning home; I hear voices that pray; I notice moments of forgiveness, and I witness many signs of hope. I don't have to wait until all is well, but I can celebrate every little hint of the Kingdom that is at hand.

This is a real discipline. It requires choosing for the light even when there is much darkness to frighten me, choosing for life even when the forces of death are so visible, and choosing for the truth even when I am surrounded with lies. I am tempted to be so impressed by the obvious sadness of the human condition that I no longer claim the joy manifesting itself in many small but very real ways. The reward of choosing joy is joy itself. Living among people with mental disabilities has convinced me of that. There is so much rejection, pain, and woundedness among us, but once you choose to claim the joy hidden in the midst of all suffering, life becomes celebration. Joy never denies the sadness, but transforms it to a fertile soil for more joy.

Surely I will be called naive, unrealistic, and sentimental, and I will be accused of ignoring the "real" problems, the structural evils that underlie much of human misery. But God rejoices when one repentant sinner returns. Statistically that is not very interesting. But for God, numbers never seem to matter. Who knows whether the world is kept from destruction because of one, two, or three people who have continued to pray when the rest of humanity has lost hope and dissipated itself?

From God's perspective, one hidden act of repentance, one little gesture of selfless love, one moment of true forgiveness is all that is needed to bring God from his throne to run to his returning son and to fill the heavens with sounds of divine joy.

Not Without Sorrow

If that is God's way, then I am challenged to let go of all the voices of doom and damnation that drag me into depression and allow the "small" joys to reveal the truth about the world I live in. When Jesus speaks about the world, he is very realistic. He speaks about wars and revolutions, earthquakes, plagues and famines, persecution and imprisonment, betrayal, hatred and assassinations. There is no suggestion at all that these signs of the world's darkness will ever be absent. But still, God's joy can be ours in the midst of it all. It is the joy of belonging to the household of God whose love is stronger than death and who empowers us to be in the world while already belonging to the kingdom of joy.

This is the secret of the joy of the saints. From St. Anthony of the desert, to St. Francis of Assisi, to Frère Roger Schultz of Taizé, to Mother Teresa of Calcutta, joy has been the mark of the people of God. That joy can be seen on the faces of the many simple, poor, and often suffering people who live today among great economic and social upheaval, but who can already hear the music and the dance in the Father's house. I, myself, see this joy every day in the faces of the mentally handicapped people of my community. All these holy men and women, whether they lived long ago or belong to our own time, can recognize the many small returns that take place every day and rejoice with the Father. They have somehow pierced the meaning of true joy.

For me it is amazing to experience daily the radical difference between cynicism and joy. Cynics seek darkness wherever they go. They point always to approaching dangers, impure motives, and hidden schemes. They call trust naive, care romantic, and forgiveness sentimental. They sneer at enthusiasm, ridicule spiritual fervor, and despise charismatic behavior. They consider themselves realists who see reality for what it truly is and who are not deceived by "escapist emotions." But in belittling God's joy, their darkness only calls forth more darkness.

People who have come to know the joy of God do not deny the darkness, but they choose not to live in it. They claim that the light that shines in the darkness can be trusted more than the darkness itself and that a little bit of light can dispel a lot of darkness. They point each other to flashes of light here and there, and remind each other that they reveal the hidden but real presence of God. They discover that there are people who heal each other's wounds, forgive each other's offenses, share their possessions, foster the spirit of community, celebrate the gifts they have received, and live in constant anticipation of the full manifestation of God's glory.

Every moment of each day I have the chance to choose between cynicism and joy. Every thought I have can be cynical or joyful.

Every word I speak can be cynical or joyful. Every action can be cynical or joyful. Increasingly I am aware of all these possible choices, and increasingly I discover that every choice for joy in turn reveals more joy and offers more reason to make life a true celebration in the house of the Father.

Jesus lived this joy of the Father's house to the full. In him we can see his Father's joy. "Everything the Father has is mine," he says, including God's boundless joy. That divine joy does not obliterate the divine sorrow. In our world, joy and sorrow exclude each other. Here below, joy means the absence of sorrow and sorrow the absence of joy. But such distinctions do not exist in God. Jesus, the Son of God, is the man of sorrows, but also the man of complete joy. We catch a glimpse of this when we realize that in the midst of his greatest suffering Jesus is never separated from his Father. His union with God is never broken even when he "feels" abandoned by God. The joy of God belongs to his sonship, and this joy of Jesus and his Father is offered to me. Jesus wants me to have the same joy he enjoys: "I have loved you, just as my Father has loved me. Remain in my love. If you keep my commandments you will remain in my love just as I have kept my Father's commandments and remain in his love. I have told you this, so that my own joy may be in you and your joy be complete."

As the returned child of God, living in the Father's house, God's joy is mine to claim. There is seldom a minute in my life that I am not tempted by sadness, melancholy, cynicism, dark moods, somber thoughts, morbid speculations, and waves of depression. And often I allow them to cover up the joy of my Father's house. But when I truly believe that I have already returned and that my Father has already dressed me with a cloak, ring, and sandals, I can remove the mask of the sadness from my heart and dispel the lie it tells about my true self and claim the truth with the inner freedom of the child of God.

But there is more. A child does not remain a child. A child becomes an adult. An adult becomes father and mother. When the prodigal son returns home, he returns not to remain a child, but to claim his sonship and become a father himself. As the returned child of God who is invited to resume my place in my Father's home, the challenge now, yes the call, is to become the Father myself. I am awed by this call. For a long time I have lived with the insight that returning to my Father's home was the ultimate call. It has taken me much spiritual work to make the elder son as well as the younger son in me turn around and receive the welcoming love of the Father. The fact is that, on many levels, I am still returning. But the closer I come to home the clearer becomes the realization that there is a call beyond the call to return. It is the call to become the Father who welcomes home and calls for a celebration. Having reclaimed my sonship, I now have to claim fatherhood. When I first saw Rembrandt's *Prodigal Son,* I could never have dreamt that becoming the repentant son was only a step on the way to becoming the welcoming father. I now see that the hands that forgive, console, heal, and offer a festive meal must become my own. Becoming the Father is, therefore, for me the surprising conclusion of these reflections on Rembrandt's *The Return of the Prodigal Son.*

CONCLUSION: BECOMING THE FATHER

.

"Be compassionate as your Father is compassionate."

A Lonely Step

When I first saw the detail of Rembrandt's *Prodigal Son,* a spiritual journey was set in motion that led me to write this book. As I now come to its conclusion, I discover how long a journey I have made.

From the beginning I was prepared to accept that not only the younger son, but also the elder son would reveal to me an important aspect of my spiritual journey. For a long time the father remained "the other," the one who would receive me, forgive me, offer me a home, and give me peace and joy. The father was the place to return to, the goal of my journey, the final resting place. It was only gradually and often quite painfully that I came to realize that my spiritual journey would never be complete as long as the father remained an outsider.

It dawned on me that even my best theological and spiritual formation had not been able to completely free me from a Father God who remained somewhat threatening and somewhat fearsome. All I had learned about the Father's love had not fully enabled me to let go of an authority above me who had power over me and would use it according to his will. Somehow, God's love for me was limited by my fear of God's power, and it seemed wise to keep a careful distance even though the desire for closeness was immense. I know that I share this experience with countless others. I have seen how the fear of becoming subject to God's revenge and punishment has paralyzed the mental and emotional lives of many people, independently of their age, religion, or life-style. This paralyzing fear of God is one of the great human tragedies.

Rembrandt's painting and his own tragic life have offered me a context in which to discover that the final stage of the spiritual life is to so fully let go of all fear of the Father that it becomes possible to become like him. As long as the Father evokes fear, he remains an outsider and cannot dwell within me. But Rembrandt, who showed me the Father in utmost vulnerability, made me come to the awareness that my final vocation is indeed to become like the Father and to live out his divine compassion in my daily life. Though I am both the younger son and the elder son, I am not to remain them, but to become the Father. No father or mother ever became father or mother without having been son or daughter, but every son and daughter has to consciously choose to step beyond their childhood and become father and mother for others. It is a hard and lonely step to take—especially in a period of history in which parenthood is so hard to live well—but it is a step that is essential for the fulfillment of the spiritual journey.

Although Rembrandt does not place the father in the physical center of his painting, it is clear that the father is the center of the event the painting portrays. From him comes all the light, to him goes all the attention. Rembrandt, faithful to the parable, intended that our primary attention go to the father before anyone else.

I am amazed at how long it has taken me to make the father the center of my attention. It was so easy to identify with the two sons. Their outer and inner waywardness is so understandable and so profoundly human that identification happens almost spontaneously as soon as the connections are pointed out. For a long time I had identified myself so fully with the younger son that it did not even occur to me that I might be more like the elder. But as soon as a friend said, "Aren't you the elder son in the story?" it was hard to see anything else. Seemingly, we all participate to a greater or lesser degree in all the forms of human brokenness. Neither greed nor anger, neither lust nor resentment, neither frivolity nor jealousy are completely absent from any one of us. Our human brokenness can be acted out in many ways, but there is no offense, crime, or war that does not have its seeds in our own hearts.

But what of the father? Why pay so much attention to the sons when it is the father who is in the center and when it is the father with whom I am to identify? Why talk so much about being like the sons when the real question is: Are you interested in being like the father? It feels somehow good to be able to say: "These sons are like me." It gives a sense of being understood. But how does it feel to say: "The father is like me"? Do I want to be like the father? Do I want to be not just the one who is being forgiven, but also the one who forgives; not just the one who is being welcomed home, but also the one who welcomes home; not just the one who receives compassion, but the one who offers it as well?

Isn't there a subtle pressure in both the Church and society to remain a dependent child? Hasn't the Church in the past stressed obedience in a fashion that made it hard to claim spiritual fatherhood, and hasn't our consumer society encouraged us to indulge in childish self-gratification? Who has truly challenged us to liberate ourselves from immature dependencies and to accept the burden of responsible adults? And aren't we ourselves constantly trying to escape the fearful task of fatherhood? Rembrandt certainly did. Only after much pain and suffering, when he approached death, was he able to understand and paint true spiritual paternity.

Perhaps the most radical statement Jesus ever made is: "Be compassionate as your Father is compassionate." God's compassion is described by Jesus not simply to show me how willing God is to feel for me, or to forgive me my sins and offer me new life and happiness, but to invite me to become like God and to show the same compassion to others as he is showing to me. If the only meaning of the story were that people sin but God forgives, I could easily begin to think of my sins as a fine occasion for God to show me his forgiveness. There would be no real challenge in such an interpretation. I would resign myself to my weaknesses and keep hoping that eventually God would close his eyes to them and let me come home, whatever I did. Such sentimental romanticism is not the message of the Gospels.

What I am called to make true is that whether I am the younger or the elder son, I am the son of my compassionate Father. I am an heir. No one says it more clearly than Paul when he writes: "The Spirit himself joins with our spirit to bear witness that we are children of God. And if we are children, then we are heirs, heirs of God and joint heirs with Christ, provided that we share his sufferings, so as to share his glory." Indeed, as son and heir I am to become successor. I am destined to step into my Father's place and offer to others the same compassion that he has offered me. The return to the Father is ultimately the challenge to become the Father.

This call to become the Father precludes any "soft" interpretation of the story. I know how much I long to return and be held safe, but do I really want to be son and heir with all that that implies? Being in the Father's house requires that I make the Father's life my own and become transformed in his image.

Recently, on looking into a mirror, I was struck by how much I look like my dad. Looking at my own features, I suddenly saw the man whom I had seen when I was twenty-seven years old: the man I had admired as well as criticized, loved as well as feared. Much of my energy had been invested in finding my own self in the face of this person, and many of my questions about who I was and who I was to become had been shaped by being the son of this man. As I suddenly saw this man appearing in the mirror, I was overcome with the awareness that all the differences I had been aware of during my lifetime seemed so small compared with the similarities. As with a shock, I realized that I was indeed heir, successor, the one who is admired, feared, praised, and misunderstood by others, as my dad was by me.

The Fatherhood of Compassion

Rembrandt's portrayal of the father of the prodigal son makes me understand that I no longer need to use my sonship to keep my distance. Having lived my sonship to its fullest, the time has come to step over all barriers and claim the truth that becoming the old man in front of me is all I really desire for myself. I cannot remain a child forever, I cannot keep pointing to my father as an excuse for my life. I have to dare to stretch out my own hands in blessing and to receive with ultimate compassion my children, regardless of how they feel or think about me. Since becoming the compassionate Father is the ultimate goal of the spiritual life, as it is expressed in the parable as well as in Rembrandt's painting, I now need to explore its full significance.

First of all, I have to keep in mind the context in which Jesus tells the story of the "man who had two sons." Luke writes: "The tax collectors and sinners . . . were all crowding around to listen to him, and the Pharisees and scribes complained saying: 'This man welcomes sinners and eats with them.' " They put his legitimacy as a teacher in question by criticizing his closeness to sinful people. In response Jesus tells his critics the parables of the lost sheep, the lost coin, and the prodigal son.

Jesus wants to make it clear that the God of whom he speaks is a God of compassion who joyously welcomes repentant sinners into his house. To associate and eat with people of ill repute, therefore, does not contradict his teaching about God, but does, in fact, live out this teaching in everyday life. If God forgives the sinners, then certainly those who have faith in God should do the same. If God welcomes sinners home, then certainly those who trust in God should do likewise. If God is compassionate, then certainly those who love God should be compassionate as well. The God whom Jesus announces and in whose name he acts is the God of compassion, the God who offers himself as example and model for all human behavior.

But there is more. Becoming like the heavenly Father is not just one important aspect of Jesus' teaching, it is the very heart of his message. The radical quality of Jesus' words and the seeming impossibility of his demands are quite obvious when heard as part of a general call to become and to be true sons and daughters of God.

As long as we belong to this world, we will remain subject to its competitive ways and expect to be rewarded for all the good we do. But when we belong to God, who loves us without conditions, we can live as he does. The great conversion called for by Jesus is to move from belonging to the world to belonging to God.

When, shortly before his death, Jesus prays to his Father for his disciples, he says: "[Father,] they do not belong to the world any more than I belong to the world. . . . May they all be one . . . just as, Father, you are in me and I am in you, so that they also may be in us, so that the world may believe it was you who sent me."

Once we are in God's house as sons and daughters of his household, we can be like him, love like him, be good like him, care like him. Jesus leaves no doubt about this when he explains that: "If you love those who love you, what credit can you expect? Even sinners love those who love them. And if you do good to those who do good to you, what credit can you expect? For even sinners do that much. And if you lend to those from whom you hope to get money back, what credit can you expect? . . . Even sinners lend to sinners to get back the same amount. Instead, love your enemies and do good to them, and lend without any hope of return. You will have a great reward, and you will be children of the Most High, for he himself is kind to the ungrateful and to the wicked. Be compassionate just as your Father is compassionate."

That is the core message of the Gospel. The way human beings are called to love one another is God's way. We are called to love one another with the same selfless outgoing love that we see in Rembrandt's depiction of the father. The compassion with which we are to love cannot be based upon a competitive life-style. It has to be this absolute compassion in which no trace of competition can be found. It has to be this radical love of enemy. If we are not only to be received by God, but also to receive as God, we must become like the heavenly Father and see the world through his eyes.

But even more important than the context of the parable and the explicit teaching of Jesus is the person of Jesus himself. Jesus is the true Son of the Father. He is the model for our becoming the Father. In him the fullness of God dwells. All the knowledge of God resides in him; all the glory of God remains in him; all the power of God belongs to him. His unity with the Father is so intimate and so complete that to see Jesus is to see the Father. "Show us the Father," Philip says to him. Jesus responds, "Anyone who has seen me has seen the Father."

Jesus shows us what true sonship is. He is the younger son without being rebellious. He is the elder son without being resentful. In everything he is obedient to the Father, but never his slave. He hears everything the Father says, but this does not make him his servant. He does everything the Father sends him to do, but remains completely free. He gives everything, and he receives everything. He declares openly: "In all truth I tell you, by himself the Son can do nothing. He can only do what he sees the Father doing; and whatever the Father does the Son does too. For the Father loves the Son and shows him everything he himself does, and he will show him even greater things than these works that will astonish you. Thus as the Father raises the dead and gives them life, so the Son gives life to anyone he chooses; for the Father judges no one; he has entrusted all judgment to the Son, so that all may honor the Son as they honor the Father."

This is divine sonship. And it is to this sonship that I am called. The mystery of redemption is that God's Son became flesh so that all the lost children of God could become sons and daughters as Jesus is son. In this perspective, the story of the prodigal son takes on a whole new dimension. Jesus, the Beloved of the Father, leaves his Father's home to take on the sins of God's wayward children and bring them home. But, while leaving, he stays close to the Father and through total obedience offers healing to his resentful brothers and sisters. Thus, for my sake, Jesus becomes the younger son as well as the elder son in order to show me how to become the Father. Through him I can become a true son again and, as a true son, I finally can grow to become compassionate as our heavenly Father is.

As the years of my life pass, I discover how arduous and challenging, but also how fulfilling it is to grow into this spiritual fatherhood. Rembrandt's painting rules out any thought that this has anything to do with power, influence, or control. I might once have held the illusion that one day the many bosses would be gone and I could finally be the boss myself. But this is the way of the world in which power is the main concern. And it is not difficult to see that those who have tried most of their lives to get rid of their bosses are not going to be very different from their predecessors when they finally step into their places. Spiritual fatherhood has nothing to do with power or control. It is a fatherhood of compassion. And I have to keep looking at the father embracing the prodigal son to catch a glimpse of this.

Against my own best intentions, I find myself continually striving to acquire power. When I give advice, I want to know whether it is being followed; when I offer help, I want to be thanked; when I give money, I want it to be used my way; when I do something good, I want to be remembered. I might not get a statue, or even a memorial plaque, but I am constantly concerned that I not be forgotten, that somehow I will live on in the thoughts and deeds of others.

But the father of the prodigal son is not concerned about himself. His long-suffering life has emptied him of his desires to keep in control of things. His children are his only concern, to them he wants to give himself completely, and for them he wants to pour out all of himself.

Can I give without wanting anything in return, love without putting any conditions on my love? Considering my immense need for human recognition and affection, I realize that it will be a lifelong struggle. But I am also convinced that each time I step over this need and act free of my concern for return, I can trust that my life can truly bear the fruits of God's Spirit.

Is there a way to this spiritual fatherhood? Or am I doomed to remain so caught up in my own need to find a place in my world that I end up ever and again using the authority of power instead of the authority of compassion? Has competition so pervaded my entire being that I will continue to see my own children as rivals? If Jesus truly calls me to be compassionate as his heavenly Father is compassionate and if Jesus offers himself as the way to that compassionate life, then I cannot keep acting as though competition is, in fact, the last word. I must trust that I am capable of becoming the Father I am called to be.

Grief, Forgiveness, and Generosity

Looking at Rembrandt's painting of the father, I can see three ways to a truly compassionate fatherhood: grief, forgiveness, and generosity.

It might sound strange to consider grief a way to compassion. But it is. Grief asks me to allow the sins of the world—my own included—to pierce my heart and make me shed tears, many tears, for them. There is no compassion without many tears. If they can't be tears that stream from my eyes, they have to be at least tears that well up from my heart. When I consider the immense waywardness of God's children, our lust, our greed, our violence, our anger, our resentment, and when I look at them through the eyes of God's heart, I cannot but weep and cry out in grief:

> Look, my soul, at the way one human being tries to inflict as much pain on another as possible; look at these people plotting to bring harm to their fellows; look at these parents molesting their children; look at this landowner exploiting his workers; look at the violated women, the misused men, the abandoned children. Look, my soul, at the world; see the concentration camps, the prisons, the nursing homes, the hospitals, and hear the cries of the poor.

This grieving is praying. There are so few mourners left in this world. But grief is the discipline of the heart that sees the sin of the world, and knows itself to be the sorrowful price of freedom without which love cannot bloom. I am beginning to see that much of praying is grieving. This grief is so deep not just because the human sin is so great, but also—and more so—because the divine love is so boundless. To become like the Father whose only authority is compassion, I have to shed countless tears and so prepare my heart to receive anyone, whatever their journey has been, and forgive them from that heart.

The second way that leads to spiritual fatherhood is forgiveness. It is through constant forgiveness that we become like the Father. Forgiveness from the heart is very, very difficult. It is next to impossible. Jesus said to his disciples: "When your brother wrongs you seven times a day and seven times comes back to you and says, 'I am sorry,' you must forgive him."

I have often said, "I forgive you," but even as I said these words my heart remained angry or resentful. I still wanted to hear the story that tells me that I was right after all; I still wanted to hear apologies and excuses; I still wanted the satisfaction of receiving some praise in return—if only the praise for being so forgiving!

But God's forgiveness is unconditional; it comes from a heart that does not demand anything for itself, a heart that is completely empty of self-seeking. It is this divine forgiveness that I have to practice in my daily life. It calls me to keep stepping over all my arguments that say forgiveness is unwise, unhealthy, and impractical. It challenges me to step over all my needs for gratitude and compliments. Finally, it demands of me that I step over that wounded part of my heart that feels hurt and wronged and that wants to stay in control and put a few conditions between me and the one whom I am asked to forgive.

This "stepping over" is the authentic discipline of forgiveness. Maybe it is more "climbing over" than "stepping over." Often I have to climb over the wall of arguments and angry feelings that I have erected between myself and all those whom I love but who so often do not return that love. It is a wall of fear of being used or hurt again. It is a wall of pride, and the desire to stay in control. But every time that I can step or climb over that wall, I enter into the house where the Father dwells, and there touch my neighbor with genuine compassionate love.

Grief allows me to see beyond my wall and realize the immense suffering that results from human lostness. It opens my heart to a genuine solidarity with my fellow humans. Forgiveness is the way to step over the wall and welcome others into my heart without expecting anything in return. Only when I remember that I am the Beloved Child can I welcome those who want to return with the same compassion as that with which the Father welcomes me.

The third way to become like the Father is generosity. In the parable, the father not only gives his departing son everything he asks, but also showers him with gifts on his return. And to his elder son he says: "All I have is yours." There is nothing the father keeps for himself. He pours himself out for his sons.

He does not simply offer more than can be reasonably expected from someone who has been offended; no, he completely gives himself away without reserve. Both sons are for him "everything." In them he wants to pour out his very life. The way the younger son is given robe, ring, and sandals, and welcomed home with a sumptuous celebration, as well as the way the elder son is urged to accept his unique place in his father's heart and to join his younger brother around the table, make it very clear that all boundaries of patriarchal behavior are broken through. This is not the picture of a remarkable father. This is the portrayal of God, whose goodness, love, forgiveness, care, joy, and compassion have no limits at all. Jesus presents God's generosity by using all the imagery that his culture provides, while constantly transforming it.

In order to become like the Father, I must be as generous as the Father is generous. Just as the Father gives his very self to his children, so must I give my very self to my brothers and sisters. Jesus makes it very clear that it is precisely this giving of self that is the mark of the true disciple. "No one can have greater love than to lay down his life for his friends."

This giving of self is a discipline because it is something that does not come spontaneously. As children of the darkness that rules through fear, self-interest, greed, and power, our great motivators are survival and self-preservation. But as children of the light who know that perfect love casts out all fear, it becomes possible to give away all that we have for others.

As children of the light, we prepare ourselves to become true martyrs: people who witness with their whole lives to the unlimited love of God. Giving all thus becomes gaining all. Jesus expresses this clearly as he says: "Anyone who loses his life for my sake . . . will save it."

Every time I take a step in the direction of generosity, I know that I am moving from fear to love. But these steps, certainly at first, are hard to take because there are so many emotions and feelings that hold me back from freely giving. Why should I give energy, time, money, and yes, even attention to someone who has offended me? Why should I share my life with someone who has shown no respect for it? I might be willing to forgive, but to give on top of that!

Still . . . the truth is that, in a spiritual sense, the one who has offended me belongs to my "kin," my "gen." The word "generosity" includes the term "gen" which we also find in the words "gender," "generation," and "generativity." This term, from the Latin *genus* and the Greek *genos,* refers to our being of one kind. Generosity is a giving that comes from the knowledge of that intimate bond. True generosity is acting on the truth—not on the feeling—that those I am asked to forgive are "kinfolk," and belong to my family. And whenever I act this way, that truth will become more visible to me. Generosity creates the family it believes in.

Grief, forgiveness, and generosity are, then, the three ways by which the image of the Father can grow in me. They are three aspects of the Father's call to *be* home. As the Father, I am no longer *called* to come home as the younger or elder son, but to *be* there as the one to whom the wayward children can return and be welcomed with joy. It is very hard to just *be* home and wait. It is a waiting in grief for those who have left and a waiting with hope to offer forgiveness and new life to those who will return.

As the Father, I have to believe that all that the human heart desires can be found at home. As the Father, I have to be free from the need to wander around curiously and to catch up with what I might otherwise perceive as missed childhood opportunities. As the Father, I have to know that, indeed, my youth is over and that playing youthful games is nothing but a ridiculous attempt to cover up the truth that I am old and close to death. As the Father, I have to dare to carry the responsibility of a spiritually adult person and dare to trust that the real joy and real fulfillment can only come from welcoming home those who have been hurt and wounded on their life's journey, and loving them with a love that neither asks nor expects anything in return.

There is a dreadful emptiness in this spiritual fatherhood. No power, no success, no popularity, no easy satisfaction. But that same dreadful emptiness is also the place of true freedom. It is the place where there is "nothing left to lose," where love has no strings attached, and where real spiritual strength is found.

Every time I touch that dreadful yet fruitful emptiness in myself, I know that I can welcome anyone there without condemnation and offer hope. There I am free to receive the burdens of others without any need to evaluate, categorize, or analyze. There, in that completely non-judgmental state of being, I can engender liberating trust.

Once, while visiting a dying friend, I directly experienced this holy emptiness. In my friend's presence I felt no desire to ask questions about the past or to speculate about the future. We were just together without fear, without guilt or shame, without worries. In that emptiness, God's unconditional love could be sensed and we could say what the old Simeon said when he took the Christ child in his arms: "Now, Master, you can let your servant go in peace as you promised." There, in the midst of the dreadful emptiness, was complete trust, complete peace, and complete joy. Death no longer was the enemy. Love was victorious.

Each time we touch that sacred emptiness of non-demanding love, heaven and earth tremble and there is great "rejoicing among the angels of God." It is the joy for the returning sons and daughters. It is the joy of spiritual fatherhood.

Living out this spiritual fatherhood requires the radical discipline of being home. As a self-rejecting person always in search of affirmation and affection, I find it impossible to love consistently without asking for something in return. But the discipline is precisely to give up wanting to accomplish this myself as a heroic feat. To claim for myself spiritual fatherhood and the authority of compassion that belongs to it, I have to let the rebellious younger son and the resentful elder son step up on the platform to receive the unconditional, forgiving love that the Father offers me, and to discover there the call to be home as my Father is home.

Then both sons in me can gradually be transformed into the compassionate father. This transformation leads me to the fulfillment of the deepest desire of my restless heart. Because what greater joy can there be for me than to stretch out my tired arms and let my hands rest in a blessing on the shoulders of my home-coming children?

EPILOGUE:
LIVING THE PAINTING

·

When I saw the Rembrandt poster for the first time in the
fall of 1983, all my attention was drawn to the hands of
the old father pressing his returning boy to his chest. I saw forgiveness, reconciliation, healing; I also saw safety, rest, being at home. I
was so deeply touched by this image of the life-giving embrace of
father and son because everything in me yearned to be received in
the way the prodigal son was received. That encounter turned out to
be the beginning of my own return.

The L'Arche community gradually became my home. Never in
my life did I dream that men and women with a mental handicap

would be the ones who would put their hands on me in a gesture of blessing and offer me a home. For a long time, I had sought safety and security among the wise and clever, hardly aware that the things of the Kingdom were revealed to "little children"; that God has chosen "those who by human standards are fools to shame the wise."

But when I experienced the warm, unpretentious reception of those who have nothing to boast about, and experienced a loving embrace from people who didn't ask any questions, I began to discover that a true spiritual homecoming means a return to the poor in spirit to whom the Kingdom of Heaven belongs. The embrace of the Father became very real to me in the embraces of the mentally poor.

Having first viewed the painting while visiting a community of mentally handicapped people allowed me to make a connection that is deeply rooted in the mystery of our salvation. It is the connection between the blessing given by God and the blessing given by the poor. In L'Arche I came to see that these blessings are truly one. The Dutch master not only brought me into touch with the deepest longings of my heart, but also led me to discover that those longings could be fulfilled in the community where I first met him.

It now has been more than six years since I first saw the Rembrandt poster at Trosly and five years since I decided to make L'Arche my home. As I reflect on these years, I realize that the people with a mental handicap and their assistants made me "live" Rembrandt's painting more completely than I could have anticipated. The warm welcomes I have received in many L'Arche houses and the many celebrations I have shared have allowed me to experience deeply the younger son's return. Welcome and celebration are, indeed, two of the main characteristics of the life "in the Ark." There are so many welcome signs, hugs and kisses, songs, skits, and festive meals that for an outsider L'Arche may appear a lifelong homecoming celebration.

I also have lived the elder son's story. I hadn't really seen how much the elder son belongs to Rembrandt's *Prodigal Son* until I went to Saint Petersburg and saw the whole picture. There I discovered the tension Rembrandt evokes. There is not only the light-filled reconciliation between the father and the younger son, but also the dark, resentful distance of the elder son. There is repentance, but also anger. There is communion, but also alienation. There is the warm glow of healing, but also the coolness of the critical eye; there is the offer of mercy, but also the enormous resistance against receiving it. It didn't take long before I encountered the elder son in me.

Life in community does not keep the darkness away. To the contrary. It seems that the light that attracted me to L'Arche also made me conscious of the darkness in myself. Jealousy, anger, the feeling of being rejected or neglected, the sense of not truly belonging—all of these emerged in the context of a community striving for a life of forgiveness, reconciliation, and healing. Community life has opened me up to the real spiritual combat: the struggle to keep moving toward the light precisely when the darkness is so real.

As long as I lived by myself, it seemed rather easy to keep the elder son hidden from view. But the sharing of life with people who are not hiding their feelings soon confronted me with the elder son within. There is little romanticism to community life. There is the constant need to keep stepping out of the engulfing darkness onto the platform of the father's embrace.

Handicapped people have little to lose. Without guile they show me who they are. They openly express their love as well as their fear, their gentleness as well as their anguish, their generosity as well as their selfishness. By just simply being who they are, they break through my sophisticated defenses and demand that I be as open with them as they are with me. Their handicap unveils my own. Their anguish mirrors my own. Their vulnerabilities show me my own. By forcing me to confront the elder son in me, L'Arche opened the way to bring him home. The same handicapped people who welcomed me home and invited me to celebrate also confronted me with my not yet converted self and made me aware that the journey was far from ended.

While these discoveries have profoundly impacted on my life, the greatest gift from L'Arche is the challenge of becoming the Father. Being older in years than most members of the community and also being its pastor, it seems natural to think of myself as a father.

Because of my ordination, I already have the title. Now I have to live up to it.

Becoming the Father in a community of mentally handicapped people and their assistants is far more demanding than grappling with the struggles of the younger and the elder son. Rembrandt's father is a father who is emptied out by suffering. Through the many "deaths" he suffered, he became completely free to receive and to give. His outstretched hands are not begging, grasping, demanding, warning, judging, or condemning. They are hands that only bless, giving all and expecting nothing.

I am now faced with the hard and seemingly impossible task of letting go of the child in me. Paul says it clearly: "When I was a child, I used to talk like a child, and see things as a child does, and think like a child; but now that I have become an adult, I have finished with all childish ways." It is comfortable to be the wayward younger son or the angry elder son.

Our community is full of wayward and angry children, and being surrounded by peers gives a sense of solidarity. Yet the longer I am part of the community, the more that solidarity proves to be only a way station on the road to a much more lonely destination: the loneliness of the Father, the loneliness of God, the ultimate loneliness of compassion. The community does not need yet another younger or elder son, whether converted or not, but a father who lives with outstretched hands, always desiring to let them rest on the shoulders of his returning children. Yet everything in me resists that vocation. I keep clinging to the child in me. I do not want to be half blind; I want to see clearly what is going on around me. I do not want to wait until my children come home; I want to be with them where they are in a foreign country or on the farm with the servants. I do not want to remain silent about what happened; I am curious to hear the whole story and have countless questions to ask. I do not want to keep stretching my hands out when there are so few who are willing to be embraced, especially when fathers and father figures are considered by many the source of their problems.

And still, after a long life as son, I know for sure that the true call is to become a father who only blesses in endless compassion, asking no questions, always giving and forgiving, never expecting anything in return. In a community, all this is often disturbingly concrete. I want to know what is happening. I want to be involved in the daily ups and downs of people's lives. I want to be remembered, invited, and informed. But the fact is that few recognize my desire and those who do are not sure how to respond to it. My people, whether handicapped or not, are not looking for another peer, another playmate, nor even for another brother. They seek a father who can bless and forgive without needing them in the way they need him. I see clearly the truth of my vocation to be a father; at the same time it seems to me almost impossible to follow it. I don't want to stay home while everyone goes out, whether driven by their many desires or their many angers. I feel these same impulses and want to run around like others do! But who is going to be home when they return—tired, exhausted, excited, disappointed, guilty, or ashamed? Who is going to convince them that, after all is said and done, there is a safe place to return to and receive an embrace? If it is not I, who is it going to be? The joy of fatherhood is vastly different from the pleasure of the wayward children. It is a joy beyond rejection and loneliness; yes, even beyond affirmation and community. It is the joy of a fatherhood that takes its name from the heavenly Father and partakes in his divine solitude.

It does not surprise me at all that few people claim fatherhood for themselves. The pains are too obvious, the joys too hidden. And still, by not claiming it I shirk my responsibility as a spiritually adult person. Yes, I even betray my vocation. Nothing less than that! But how can I choose what seems so contrary to all my needs? A voice says to me, "Don't be afraid. The Child will take you by the hand and lead you to fatherhood." I know that voice can be trusted. As always, the poor, the weak, the marginal, the rejected, the forgotten, the least . . . they not only need me to be their father, but also show me how to be a father for them. True fatherhood is sharing the poverty of God's non-demanding love. I am afraid to enter into that poverty, but those who have already entered it through their physical or mental disabilities will be my teachers.

Looking at the people I live with, the handicapped men and women as well as their assistants, I see the immense desire for a father in whom fatherhood and motherhood are one. They all have suffered from the experience of rejection or abandonment; they all have been wounded as they grew up; they all wonder whether they are worthy of the unconditional love of God, and they all search for the place where they can safely return and be touched by hands that bless them.

Rembrandt portrays the father as the man who has transcended the ways of his children. His own loneliness and anger may have been there, but they have been transformed by suffering and tears. His loneliness has become endless solitude, his anger boundless gratitude. This is who I have to become. I see it as clearly as I see the immense beauty of the father's emptiness and compassion. Can I let the younger and the elder son grow in me to the maturity of the compassionate father?

When, four years ago, I went to Saint Petersburg to see Rembrandt's *The Return of the Prodigal Son,* I had little idea how much I would have to live what I then saw. I stand with awe at the place where Rembrandt brought me. He led me from the kneeling, disheveled young son to the standing, bent-over old father, from the place of being blessed to the place of blessing. As I look at my own aging hands, I know that they have been given to me to stretch out toward all who suffer, to rest upon the shoulders of all who come, and to offer the blessing that emerges from the immensity of God's love.

NOTES

∎

Chapter 2

"was dead and has . . . lost and is found"
(Luke 15:32)   p. 34

For over fifteen . . . father to die
Kenneth E. Bailey, *Poet and Peasant and Through Peasant Eyes:*
A Literary-Cultural Approach to the Parables (Grand
Rapids, Mich.: William B. Eerdmans, 1983), 161–62   p. 35

"After signing over . . . underlies both requests"
Ibid., 164   p. 36

"The moment of . . . but lasts forever"
Christian Tümpel (with contributions by Astrid Tümpel),
Rembrandt (Amsterdam: N. J. W. Becht-Amsterdam,
1986), 350. Author's translation   p. 37

"The group of . . . death into life"
Jakob Rosenberg, op. cit., 231, 234   p. 37

"fashioned me in . . . my mother's womb"
(Psalm 139:13–15)   p. 37

"I can walk . . . would I fear"
(Psalm 23:4)   p. 39

"cure the sick . . . cast out devils" "received without
charge" "give without charge"
(Matthew 10:8)   p. 39

"They do not belong . . . consecrated in truth"
(John 17:16–19)   p. 39

Sensing the touch . . . touch was voice
(See I Kings 19:11–13)   p. 40

Chapter 3

"I am offering . . . holding fast to him"
(Deuteronomy 30:19–20)   p. 50

"it was very good"
(Genesis 1:31)   p. 51

". . . grace is always greater"
(See Romans 5:20)   p. 52

"Unless you turn . . . Kingdom of Heaven"
(Matthew 18:3)   p. 53

"In all truth I tell you . . . born from above."
(John 3:3)   p. 55

"lamb of God . . . of the world"
(John 1:29)   p. 55–56

Isn't he the innocent . . . for us
(II Corinthians 5:21)   p. 56

"cling to his equality . . . human beings are"
(Philippians 2:6–7)   p. 56

"My God, my God . . . forsaken me?"
(Matthew 27:46)   p. 56

The one who told the story . . . made us part of
his fullness
(See John 1:1–14)   p. 56

drawn all people . . . home to his heavenly Father
(See John 12:32)   p. 56

"God wanted all . . . everything on earth"
(Colossians 1:19–20)   p. 56

He, who is born . . . blood of the Lamb
Pierre Marie (Frère), "Les fils prodigues et le fils prodigue,"

Sources Vives 13, Communion de Jerusalem, Paris (March 87), 87–93. Author's translation   p. 56–57

". . . we are already . . . he really is"
(I John 3:2)   p. 58

Chapter 4

Barbara Joan Haeger, "The Religious Significance of Rembrandt's Return of the Prodigal Son: An Examination of the Picture in the Context of the Visual and Iconographic Tradition."
Ph.D. diss., University of Michigan (Ann Arbor, Mich.: University Microfilm International, 1983), 173   p. 63

"not to the . . . the biblical text"
Ibid., 178   p. 63

"inner drama of the soul"
Ibid., 178   p. 64

"bitter revengeful person . . . in his way"
Gary Schwartz, *Rembrandt: zign Leven, zign Schilderijen* (Maarsen, Netherlands: Uitgeverij Gary Schwartz, 1984), 362. Author's translation   p. 65

"collect testimony . . . an insane asylum"
Charles L. Mee, *Rembrandt's Portrait: A Biography* (New York: Simon and Schuster, 1988), 229   p. 65

"Rembrandt hired . . . stayed locked up"
Ibid.   p. 65

Chapter 5

"Do not be . . . born from above"
(John 3:7)   p. 76

Chapter 6

Chapter 8

Chapter 9

Conclusion

"Now, Master, you can . . . as you promised"
(Luke 15:10)   p. 133

"rejoicing among the angels of God"
(Luke 15:10)   p. 133

Epilogue

"little children"
(Matthew 11:25)   p. 135

"those who by . . . shame the wise"
(I Corinthians 1:27)   p. 135

"When I was . . . all childish ways"
(I Corinthians 13:11)   p. 137

It is the joy of a fatherhood . . . from the heavenly
Father
(See Ephesians 3:14)   p. 138

ACKNOWLEDGMENTS

•

W hen I think of the many people who have supported me during the writing of this book, the first two who come to mind are Connie Ellis and Conrad Wieczorek. Connie Ellis has lived through all the stages of the manuscript. Her enthusiastic, dedicated, and competent secretarial help has not only kept me moving during very busy times, but also kept me trusting in the value of what I was doing during moments of discouragement. Conrad Wieczorek has offered me indispensable assistance from the early beginnings of the book until its completion. I am deeply grateful for the generosity with which he made his time and energy available to edit the text and make suggestions for changes in form and content.

Many other friends have played an important role in the reworking of this book. Elizabeth Buckley, Brad Colby, Ivan Dyer, Bart Gavigan, Jeff Imbach, Don McNeill, Sue Mosteller, Glenn Peckover, Jim Purdie, Esther de Waal, and Susan Zimmerman have all offered significant contributions. Many of the refinements are the direct result of their advice.

A very special word of thanks goes to Richard White. The generosity with which he offered me his personal support and professional expertise gave me the necessary incentive to bring this book to its final form.

Finally, I want to express my special gratitude to three friends who died before the publication of the book: Murray McDonnell, David Osler, and Madame Pauline Vanier. Murray's personal and financial support, David's friendship and warm response to the first draft, and Madame Vanier's hospitality during the time of writing, all have been a source of great encouragement to me. I miss their presence very much, but know that their love is much stronger than death and will continue to inspire me.

It fills me with great joy that I can think of this book as a true fruit of friendship and love.